CHICKEN
RECIPES

pil
Publications International, Ltd.

Let's get social!
 @Publications_International
 @PublicationsInternational
www.pilbooks.com

TABLE OF CONTENTS

AMAZING APPETIZERS

OVEN-BAKED SPICY WINGS

Makes 8 appetizer servings

2 pounds chicken wings

3 tablespoons COUNTRY CROCK® Calcium plus Vitamin D, melted

2 tablespoons red wine vinegar

1 to 2 tablespoons cayenne pepper sauce

1 Preheat oven to 450°F. Cut tips off wings (save tips for soup). Cut wings in half at joint. Arrange chicken wings in roasting pan or broiler pan without the rack. Bake 50 minutes or until chicken is thoroughly cooked and crisp.

2 Combine remaining ingredients in large bowl; add cooked chicken and toss to coat. Serve, if desired, with WISH-BONE® Chunky Blue Cheese Dressing.

NOTE: Oven-baking is easier and less messy than frying these classic appetizers.

STUFFED MUSHROOMS WITH CHICKEN SAUSAGE & FENNEL

Makes 6 servings

18 large brown mushrooms (about 2 inches in diameter)

2 teaspoons olive oil

¾ cup finely chopped fennel (about 3¼ ounces), tops reserved

2 cloves garlic, minced

½ teaspoon dried thyme

¼ teaspoon kosher salt

½ teaspoon black pepper

1 package (12 ounces) fully cooked smoked chicken apple sausage links, finely chopped

4 ounces cream cheese, softened

½ cup grated Parmesan cheese, divided

4 tablespoons Italian-style dry bread crumbs, divided

1 cup chicken broth

Fresh fennel fronds (optional)

1 Preheat oven to 375°F. Clean mushrooms with damp paper towel. Remove and chop stems.

2 Heat oil in medium skillet over medium heat. Add chopped fennel; cook and stir 3 minutes or until softened. Add garlic, thyme, salt and pepper; cook and stir 1 minute. Add sausage and mushroom stems; cook 7 to 8 minutes or until sausage is lightly browned, stirring occasionally. Remove from heat.

3 Chop reserved fennel tops. Add cream cheese, ¼ cup Parmesan, 2 tablespoons bread crumbs and 1 tablespoon finely chopped fennel tops to sausage mixture; mix well. (Discard remaining chopped fennel tops or save for another use).

4 Spray mushroom caps with nonstick cooking spray. Sprinkle lightly with additional salt and pepper. Fill each mushroom cap with about 1 tablespoon filling; place in 15×10-inch jelly-roll pan or two 13×9-inch baking dishes. Pour broth around mushrooms; sprinkle with remaining ¼ cup Parmesan and 2 tablespoons bread crumbs.

5 Bake 20 to 25 minutes or until mushrooms are golden brown. Let stand 5 minutes before serving. Garnish with fennel fronds, if desired.

QUICK CHICKEN QUESADILLAS

Makes 8 appetizer servings

4   boneless skinless chicken breasts

3   tablespoons vegetable oil, divided

½   teaspoon salt

1   large yellow onion, thinly sliced

8   (6- to 8-inch) flour tortillas

3   cups (12 ounces) shredded mild Cheddar or Monterey Jack cheese

Salsa, sour cream and/or guacamole (optional)

1 Flatten chicken breasts; cut into 1×¼-inch strips.

2 Heat 2 tablespoons oil in large skillet over high heat. Add chicken; cook 3 to 4 minutes or until lightly browned and cooked through, stirring occasionally. Season with salt. Remove to plate.

3 Add onion to skillet; cook and stir 5 minutes or until translucent. Remove to plate.

4 Heat remaining 1 tablespoon oil in same skillet. Place 1 tortilla in skillet; top with one quarter of chicken, onion and cheese. Place second tortilla over filling; press down lightly. Cook quesadilla 2 minutes per side or until browned and crisp. Repeat with remaining tortillas and filling.

5 Cut into wedges; serve with desired toppings.

NOTE: Be creative and use your own favorite fillings!

FRIED CHICKEN FINGERS WITH DIPPING SAUCE

Makes 4 servings

Dipping Sauce

- ¼ cup plain yogurt
- 2 tablespoons honey
- 2 tablespoons prepared mustard
- ¼ to ½ teaspoon ground cinnamon
- 1 tablespoon sugar
- 2 teaspoons cider vinegar
- ⅛ teaspoon salt
- ⅛ teaspoon ground red pepper

Chicken

- 1½ cups panko bread crumbs
- 1 teaspoon paprika
- ½ teaspoon garlic powder
- ½ teaspoon salt, divided
- ¼ teaspoon black pepper
- ⅓ cup buttermilk
- 1 egg
- 8 chicken tenders (about 1¼ pounds)
- 2 tablespoons vegetable oil

1 Combine sauce ingredients in small bowl; set aside.

2 Place panko in shallow dish. Combine paprika, garlic powder, ¼ teaspoon salt and pepper in another small bowl. Whisk buttermilk and egg in medium bowl. Add chicken and toss until well coated.

3 Coat chicken with panko, one piece at a time, pressing down lightly to adhere. Place on plate. Repeat with remaining chicken. Sprinkle chicken evenly with half of paprika mixture.

4 Heat oil in large skillet over medium-high heat. Place chicken in skillet, seasoned side down. Sprinkle with remaining paprika mixture. Immediately reduce heat to medium and cook 6 minutes on each side or until no longer pink in center.

5 Sprinkle chicken with remaining ¼ teaspoon salt, if desired, and serve with sauce.

MOROCCAN CHICKEN TURNOVERS

Makes 8 turnovers

½ cup (1 stick) plus 2 tablespoons butter, divided

⅔ cup finely chopped onions

½ cup finely chopped carrots

1½ teaspoons grated fresh ginger

½ teaspoon salt

½ teaspoon dried oregano

½ teaspoon ground cumin

¼ teaspoon paprika

⅛ teaspoon ground red pepper

⅓ cup water

¼ cup tomato paste

2 cups finely chopped cooked chicken

16 sheets frozen phyllo dough, thawed

Fresh cilantro sprigs (optional)

1 Melt 2 tablespoons butter in medium skillet over medium heat. Add onions and carrots; cook 6 to 8 minutes or until very soft, stirring frequently. Add ginger, salt, oregano, cumin, paprika and red pepper; cook and stir 1 minute. Stir in water and tomato paste until well blended. Add chicken; cook and stir 2 minutes. (Mixture will be very thick.) Spread filling in shallow pan; place in freezer 15 minutes to cool. (Filling may be prepared up to 24 hours in advance; store covered in refrigerator.)

2 Preheat oven to 350°F. Melt remaining ½ cup butter. Stack 4 sheets phyllo on work surface or large cutting board, brushing each with melted butter before adding next sheet. Cut phyllo stack in half lengthwise.

3 Place ¼ cup cooled filling about 1 inch from bottom of each strip. Fold one corner of phyllo diagonally across to opposite edge to form triangle; continue to fold triangle up as you would fold a flag. Arrange triangles seam side down, at least 1 inch apart, on ungreased baking sheet; brush tops with melted butter. Repeat with remaining phyllo, chicken filling and melted butter.

4 Bake 20 to 22 minutes or until golden brown. Garnish with cilantro.

TIP: To make smaller appetizers, cut each stack of phyllo crosswise into four strips and use 1 to 2 tablespoons filling for each triangle. Brush with butter and fold up triangles as directed above. Bake at 350°F 15 minutes or until golden brown.

CHICKEN FAJITA NACHOS

Makes 4 servings

2 tablespoons vegetable oil, divided

2 red bell peppers, cut into thin strips

1 large onion, cut in half and thinly sliced

2 tablespoons fajita seasoning mix (from 1¼-ounce package), divided

2 tablespoons water, divided

1 large boneless skinless chicken breast (about 12 ounces), cut into 2×1-inch strips

4 cups tortilla chips (about 30 chips)

½ cup (2 ounces) shredded Cheddar cheese

½ cup (2 ounces) shredded Monterey Jack cheese

1 jalapeño pepper, seeded and thinly sliced

1 cup shredded lettuce

½ cup salsa

Sour cream and guacamole (optional)

1 Heat 1 tablespoon oil in large skillet over medium-high heat. Add bell peppers and onion; cook 5 minutes or until tender and browned in spots, stirring frequently. Remove to large bowl; stir in 1 tablespoon fajita seasoning mix and 1 tablespoon water.

2 Heat remaining 1 tablespoon oil in same skillet over medium-high heat. Add chicken; cook 7 to 10 minutes or until cooked through, stirring occasionally. Add remaining 1 tablespoon fajita seasoning mix and 1 tablespoon water; cook and stir 3 to 5 minutes or until chicken is coated.

3 Preheat broiler. Spread chips in 11×7-inch baking dish or pan; top with vegetables, chicken, Cheddar and Monterey Jack cheeses and jalapeño.

4 Broil 2 to 4 minutes or until cheeses are melted. Top with lettuce and salsa; serve with sour cream and guacamole, if desired.

TANGY BAKED WINGS

Makes 12 servings

1 **envelope (about 1 ounce) dry onion soup and recipe mix**

⅓ **cup honey**

2 **tablespoons spicy-brown mustard**

18 **chicken wings (about 3 pounds)**

1 Stir the soup mix, honey and mustard in a large bowl.

2 Cut off the chicken wing ends and discard. Cut the chicken wings in half at the joint. Add the chicken to the soup mixture and toss to coat. Place the chicken into a large shallow-sided baking pan.

3 Bake at 400°F for 45 minutes or until the chicken is cooked through, turning over once halfway through cooking time.

BAKED EGG ROLLS

Makes 6 servings

Sesame Dipping Sauce (recipe follows)

1 ounce dried shiitake mushrooms

1 large carrot, shredded

1 can (8 ounces) sliced water chestnuts, drained and minced

3 green onions, minced

3 tablespoons chopped fresh cilantro

12 ounces ground chicken

2 tablespoons minced fresh ginger

6 cloves garlic, minced

2 tablespoons soy sauce

2 teaspoons water

1 teaspoon cornstarch

12 wonton wrappers

1 tablespoon vegetable oil

1 teaspoon sesame seeds

1 Prepare Sesame Dipping Sauce; set aside.

2 Place mushrooms in small bowl. Cover with warm water; let stand 30 minutes or until tender. Rinse well; drain, squeezing out excess water. Cut off and discard stems; finely chop caps. Combine mushrooms, carrot, water chestnuts, green onions and cilantro in large bowl.

3 Spray medium skillet with nonstick cooking spray; heat over medium-high heat. Brown chicken 2 minutes, stirring to break up meat. Add ginger and garlic; cook and stir 2 minutes or until chicken is cooked through. Add to mushroom mixture. Sprinkle with soy sauce; mix thoroughly.

4 Preheat oven to 425°F. Spray baking sheet with cooking spray; set aside. Stir 2 teaspoons water into cornstarch in small bowl. Lay 1 wonton wrapper on work surface. Spoon about ⅓ cup filling across center of wrapper to within about ½ inch of sides. Fold bottom of wrapper over filling. Fold in sides. Brush ½-inch strip across top edge with cornstarch mixture; roll up and seal securely. Place seam side down on baking sheet. Repeat with remaining wrappers.

5 Brush egg rolls with oil. Sprinkle with sesame seeds. Bake 18 minutes or until golden and crisp. Serve with Sesame Dipping Sauce.

SESAME DIPPING SAUCE
Makes about ½ cup

¼ cup rice vinegar

4 teaspoons soy sauce

2 teaspoons minced fresh ginger

1 teaspoon dark sesame oil

Combine vinegar, soy sauce, ginger and sesame oil in small bowl; stir to blend.

BAKED BUFFALO CHICKEN DIP

Makes 2 cups

- 1 container (8 ounces) cream cheese spread
- ¼ cup crumbled blue cheese
- 2 cups chopped cooked chicken breast (about 8 ounces)
- 3 tablespoons mayonnaise
- 3 tablespoons sour cream
- ¼ to ½ cup hot pepper sauce
- 1 cup (4 ounces) shredded Monterey Jack cheese
- 2 tablespoons panko bread crumbs
- Assorted vegetable sticks and/or pita chips

1 Preheat oven to 400°F. Spray 1-quart casserole with nonstick cooking spray.

2 Combine cream cheese and blue cheese in medium saucepan; heat over medium heat until melted. Remove from heat. Stir in chicken, mayonnaise, sour cream and hot pepper sauce until combined.

3 Spread chicken mixture in prepared casserole. Sprinkle with Monterey Jack cheese; top evenly with panko. Spray with cooking spray.

4 Bake 20 minutes or until lightly browned and heated through. Serve with assorted vegetable sticks and/or pita chips.

APRICOT CHICKEN POT STICKERS

Makes 10 servings

Sweet and Sour Sauce (recipe follows)

2 cups plus 1 tablespoon water, divided

2 boneless skinless chicken breasts (about 4 ounces each)

2 cups chopped finely shredded cabbage

½ cup apricot fruit spread

2 green onions, finely chopped

2 teaspoons soy sauce

½ teaspoon grated fresh ginger

⅛ teaspoon black pepper

30 (3-inch) wonton wrappers

Shredded or matchstick carrots (optional)

1 Prepare Sweet and Sour Sauce; set aside.

2 Bring 2 cups water to a boil in medium saucepan. Add chicken; reduce heat to low. Cover and simmer 10 minutes or until chicken is no longer pink. Drain; set aside.

3 Combine cabbage and remaining 1 tablespoon water in same saucepan; cook over high heat 1 to 2 minutes or until water is evaporated, stirring occasionally. Remove from heat; cool slightly.

4 Finely chop chicken; return to saucepan. Add fruit spread, green onions, soy sauce, ginger and pepper; mix well.

5 Working with one at a time, spoon slightly rounded tablespoonful chicken mixture into center of 1 wonton wrapper; brush edges lightly with water. Bring corners to center; press to seal. Repeat with remaining wrappers and filling.

6 Spray steamer basket with nonstick cooking spray. Place in large saucepan or wok. Add water to depth of about ½ inch below steamer basket. (Water should not touch steamer.) Remove steamer. Cover; bring water to a boil over high heat. Fill steamer with pot stickers, leaving space between so pot stickers do not touch. Carefully place steamer in saucepan. Steam, covered, 5 minutes. Remove to serving plate. Repeat with remaining pot stickers, if necessary. Serve with Sweet and Sour Sauce.

SWEET AND SOUR SAUCE

Makes about 1¼ cups

1 cup apricot fruit spread

¼ cup cider or white vinegar

2 tablespoons packed brown sugar

½ to 1 teaspoon dry mustard

½ teaspoon ground ginger

Combine fruit spread, vinegar, brown sugar, mustard and ginger in small saucepan; cook and stir 2 to 3 minutes over low heat until sugar is melted; remove from heat. Cool completely.

HONEY MUSTARD CHICKEN BITES

Makes about 40 appetizers

1½ pounds skinless, boneless chicken breast halves, cut into 1-inch pieces

1 jar (12 ounces) refrigerated honey mustard salad dressing

2 cups PEPPERIDGE FARM® Herb Seasoned Stuffing, crushed

2 tablespoons orange juice

1 Dip the chicken into ¾ **cup** of the dressing. Coat with the stuffing.

2 Put the chicken on a baking sheet. Bake at 400°F. for 15 minutes or until the chicken is cooked through.

3 Stir the remaining dressing and orange juice in a 1-quart saucepan over medium heat. Cook and stir until hot. Serve with the chicken for dipping.

KITCHEN TIP: To microwave dip, mix remaining dressing and orange juice in microwavable bowl. Microwave on HIGH 1 minute or until hot.

SZECHUAN CHICKEN CUCUMBER CUPS

Makes 10 servings

1½ cups finely shredded or chopped skinless rotisserie chicken

1 tablespoon rice vinegar

1 tablespoon soy sauce

1½ teaspoons dark sesame oil

1 teaspoon grated fresh ginger

⅛ teaspoon red pepper flakes

1 large seedless cucumber (about 1 pound)

¼ cup chopped fresh cilantro

1 Combine chicken, vinegar, soy sauce, sesame oil, ginger and red pepper flakes in medium bowl; mix well.

2 Trim off ends of cucumber. Use fork to score all sides of cucumber lengthwise (or peel lengthwise in alternating strips). Cut crosswise into 20 (½-inch) slices. Use melon baller or grapefruit spoon to scoop out indentation in one cut side of each slice to form cup.

3 Mound 1 tablespoon chicken mixture in each cucumber cup; sprinkle with cilantro. Serve immediately or cover and refrigerate until ready to serve.

MINI CHICKEN CHILICHANGAS WITH SALSA VERDE DIPPING SAUCE

Makes 18 appetizers

Dipping Sauce

- 1 cup ORTEGA® Salsa Verde
- ¼ cup sour cream

Chilichangas

- 1 tablespoon olive oil
- 1 pound ground chicken
- 1 cup ORTEGA® Thick & Chunky Salsa, medium
- 1 tablespoon ORTEGA® Reduced Sodium Chili Seasoning Mix
- 1 cup ORTEGA® Refried Beans
- 18 egg roll wrappers
- 1 cup (4 ounces) finely shredded Cheddar cheese

Vegetable or canola oil (for frying)

COMBINE salsa verde and sour cream in small bowl. Cover and refrigerate.

HEAT olive oil in medium skillet over medium heat until hot. Add chicken; cook and stir 5 minutes or until no longer pink. Stir in salsa and seasoning mix; cook and stir 3 minutes. Remove from heat; stir in beans. Spread mixture on baking sheet or platter to cool.

PLACE one egg roll wrapper on clean work surface. Moisten edges with water. Spoon 2 tablespoons chicken mixture across center of wrapper; sprinkle with about 1 tablespoon cheese. Fold bottom of wrapper up over filling; fold sides over filling. Moisten top edge with water again. Roll enclosed filling toward top, pressing firmly to seal. Repeat with wrappers and filling.

HEAT vegetable oil in large saucepan to 350°F. Carefully add chilichangas. Cook 3 to 5 minutes or until golden brown. Remove with slotted spoon. Drain on paper towels. Serve with dipping sauce.

TIP: To save time, you can prepare both the dipping sauce and the chilichangas ahead of time and refrigerate them. To keep the chilichangas nice and crispy, fry them just before serving.

SPICY KOREAN CHICKEN WINGS

Makes 6 to 8 servings

2 tablespoons peanut oil, plus additional for frying

2 tablespoons grated fresh ginger

½ cup soy sauce

¼ cup cider vinegar

¼ cup honey

¼ cup chili garlic sauce

2 tablespoons orange juice

1 tablespoon dark sesame oil

18 chicken wings or drummettes

Sesame seeds (optional)

1 Heat 2 tablespoons peanut oil in medium skillet over medium-high heat. Add ginger; cook and stir 1 minute. Add soy sauce, vinegar, honey, chili garlic sauce, orange juice and sesame oil; cook and stir 2 minutes.

2 Heat 2 inches of peanut oil in large heavy saucepan over medium-high heat to 350° to 375°F; adjust heat to maintain temperature.

3 Rinse wings under cold water; pat dry with paper towels. Remove and discard wing tips.

4 Add wings to oil and cook 8 to 10 minutes or until crispy and browned and chicken is cooked through. Remove to paper towel-lined plate.

5 Add wings to sauce; toss to coat. Sprinkle with sesame seeds, if desired.

CHICKEN FLAUTAS

Makes 6 servings

2 tablespoons olive oil

1 onion, diced

½ of (1½- to 2-pound) cooked rotisserie chicken, bones removed and meat shredded

½ cup ORTEGA® Salsa, any variety

6 ORTEGA® Flour Soft Tortillas

½ cup canola oil

HEAT olive oil in skillet over medium-high heat until hot. Add onions; cook and stir until tender. Add shredded chicken and salsa; toss together. Remove from heat.

PLACE several tablespoons of chicken mixture in middle of tortilla and firmly roll like a cigar. Keep tortilla roll closed with 2 toothpicks. Repeat with remaining tortillas.

HEAT canola oil in skillet over medium-high heat until hot. Fry tortilla rolls in oil for several minutes in small batches until tortillas begin to brown. Turn over and continue frying until all sides are browned, about 4 minutes. Remove tortilla rolls from oil and drain on paper towels.

REMOVE toothpicks and cut each flauta on the bias to serve.

SANDWICHES AND WRAPS

FIESTA CHICKEN SANDWICH

Makes 4 servings

2 tablespoons olive oil, plus additional for brushing sandwiches

1 small onion, sliced

1 medium red bell pepper, sliced

12 ounces chicken tenders, cut in half lengthwise and crosswise

1 cup guacamole

4 slices (1 ounce each) pepper jack cheese

2 packages (10 ounces each) 8-inch mini pizza crusts (8 crusts total)

1 Heat 2 tablespoons oil in large nonstick skillet over medium-high heat. Add onion and bell pepper; cook and stir 3 to 4 minutes or until crisp-tender. Remove vegetables with slotted spoon; set aside. Add chicken to skillet; cook and stir 4 minutes or until chicken is cooked through. Remove from skillet; wipe skillet with paper towel.

2 Layer guacamole, chicken, vegetables and cheese evenly on 4 pizza crusts; top with remaining 4 pizza crusts. Brush sandwiches lightly with additional oil.

3 Heat same skillet over medium heat. Add sandwiches in batches; cook 4 to 5 minutes per side or until cheese melts and sandwiches are golden brown. Cut into wedges to serve.

CHICKEN, HUMMUS AND VEGETABLE WRAPS

Makes 4 servings

¾ cup hummus (regular, roasted red pepper or roasted garlic)

4 (8- to 10-inch) sun-dried tomato or spinach wraps *or* whole wheat tortillas

2 cups chopped cooked chicken breast

Chipotle hot pepper sauce or Louisiana-style hot pepper sauce (optional)

½ cup shredded carrots

½ cup chopped unpeeled cucumber

½ cup thinly sliced radishes

2 tablespoons chopped fresh mint or basil

Spread hummus evenly over wraps. Arrange chicken over hummus; sprinkle with hot pepper sauce, if desired. Top with carrots, cucumber, radishes and mint. Roll up tightly. Cut in half diagonally.

VARIATION: Substitute alfalfa sprouts for the radishes.

BARBECUED CHICKEN SANDWICHES

Makes 4 servings

1 tablespoon butter

1 small green pepper, chopped (about ½ cup) (optional)

1 small onion, chopped (about ¼ cup)

¼ cup chopped celery

½ cup barbecue sauce

2 cans (4.5 ounces **each**) SWANSON® Premium White Chunk Chicken Breast in Water, drained

4 PEPPERIDGE FARM® Classic Sandwich Buns with Sesame Seeds, split and toasted

1 Heat the butter in a 2-quart saucepan over medium heat. Stir the green pepper, onion and celery in the saucepan and cook until tender.

2 Stir the barbecue sauce and chicken in the saucepan. Heat until the mixture is hot and bubbling. Divide the chicken mixture among the buns.

ASIAN CILANTRO WRAPS

Makes 4 servings

2 tablespoons raspberry or strawberry fruit spread

2 tablespoons soy sauce

⅛ teaspoon red pepper flakes

2 teaspoons canola oil

3 cups thinly sliced purple cabbage

6 ounces asparagus spears, trimmed and cut into ½-inch pieces (about 1½ cups)

½ cup thinly sliced carrots

1 cup chopped green onions, green and white parts (about 8 green onions)

4 (6-inch) flour tortillas, warmed

¼ cup chopped fresh cilantro

¼ cup chopped peanuts

1 cup diced cooked chicken breast

1 Microwave fruit spread in small microwavable bowl on HIGH 15 seconds or until slightly melted. Stir in soy sauce and red pepper flakes; set aside.

2 Heat oil in large nonstick skillet over medium-high heat. Add cabbage, asparagus and carrots; cook and stir 2 minutes. Add green onions; cook and stir 2 to 3 minutes or until cabbage is slightly wilted. Remove from heat.

3 Spoon about 1 cup filling on each tortilla. Top each evenly with sauce, cilantro, peanuts and chicken. Roll up to enclose filling.

CHICKEN AND MOZZARELLA MELTS

Makes 4 servings

2 cloves garlic, crushed

4 boneless skinless chicken breasts (about 1 pound)

Salt and black pepper

1 tablespoon pesto

4 hard rolls, split

12 fresh spinach leaves

8 fresh basil leaves*

3 plum tomatoes, sliced

½ cup (2 ounces) shredded part-skim mozzarella cheese

*Omit basil leaves if fresh are unavailable. Do not substitute dried basil leaves.

1 Preheat oven to 350°F. Rub garlic on all surfaces of chicken. Spray medium skillet with nonstick cooking spray; heat over medium heat. Add chicken; cook 5 to 6 minutes on each side or until no longer pink in center. Season with salt and pepper.

2 Brush pesto onto bottom halves of rolls; layer with spinach, basil and tomatoes. Place chicken in rolls; sprinkle cheese evenly over chicken. Top with bacon. (If desired, sandwiches may be prepared up to this point and wrapped in foil. Refrigerate until ready to bake. Bake in preheated 350°F oven until chicken is warm, about 20 minutes.)

3 Wrap sandwiches in foil; bake 10 minutes or until cheese is melted.

CHEESY CHICKEN AND BACON MELTS: Cook 8 slices bacon in large skillet. Cook garlic-rubbed chicken in 1 tablespoon drippings. Prepare as directed above. Serve in wheat French rolls.

GRILLED ITALIAN CHICKEN PANINI

Makes 6 sandwiches

6 small portobello mushroom caps (about 6 ounces)

½ cup plus 2 tablespoons balsamic vinaigrette dressing

1 loaf (16 ounces) Italian bread, cut into 12 slices

12 slices provolone cheese

1½ cups chopped cooked chicken

1 jar (12 ounces) roasted red peppers, drained

1 Brush mushrooms with 2 tablespoons dressing. Cook mushrooms in large nonstick skillet over medium-high heat 5 to 7 minutes or until soft. Cut diagonally into ½-inch slices.

2 For each sandwich, top 1 bread slice with 1 cheese slice, ¼ cup chicken, mushrooms, roasted red peppers, another cheese slice and another bread slice. Brush outsides of sandwiches with remaining dressing.

3 Preheat grill pan and panini press* at medium heat 5 minutes. Grill sandwiches 4 to 6 minutes or until cheese is melted and bread is golden, turning once during cooking.

*If you don't have a grill pan and panini press, grill sandwiches in a nonstick skillet. Place a clean heavy pan on top of sandwiches to weigh them down while cooking.

TIP: A rotisserie chicken will yield just enough chopped chicken for this recipe.

CHICKEN LETTUCE WRAPS

Makes 6 to 8 servings

1 tablespoon vegetable oil

1 small onion, finely chopped

5 ounces cremini mushrooms, finely chopped (about 2 cups)

1 pound ground chicken

¼ cup hoisin sauce

2 tablespoons soy sauce

1 tablespoon rice vinegar

1 tablespoon sriracha sauce

1 tablespoon oyster sauce

2 cloves garlic, minced

1 teaspoon grated fresh ginger

1 teaspoon dark sesame oil

½ cup finely chopped water chestnuts

2 green onions, thinly sliced

1 head butter lettuce

1 Heat vegetable oil in large skillet over medium-high heat. Add onion; cook and stir 2 minutes. Add mushrooms; cook 8 minutes or until lightly browned and liquid has evaporated, stirring occasionally.

2 Add chicken; cook 8 minutes or until no longer pink, stirring to break up meat. Stir in hoisin sauce, soy sauce, vinegar, sriracha, oyster sauce, garlic, ginger and sesame oil; cook 4 minutes. Add water chestnuts; cook and stir 2 minutes or until heated through. Remove from heat; stir in green onions.

3 Separate lettuce leaves. Spoon about ¼ cup chicken mixture into each lettuce leaf. Serve immediately.

SPICY CHICKEN SANDWICH

Makes 4 servings

2 boneless skinless chicken breasts (about 8 ounces each)

1½ cups buttermilk

3 tablespoons hot pepper sauce, divided

1 teaspoon salt

⅓ cup mayonnaise

1 teaspoon Cajun seasoning

Canola or vegetable oil for frying

1 cup all-purpose flour

½ cup cornstarch

2 teaspoons paprika

1½ teaspoons black pepper

1 teaspoon msg

1 teaspoon ground red pepper

4 brioche sandwich buns, toasted and buttered

12 to 16 dill pickle slices

1 Pound chicken to ½-inch thickness between two sheets of waxed paper or plastic wrap with rolling pin or meat mallet. Cut each breast in half crosswise to create total of four pieces. Cut off pointed ends if necessary for more even rectangular shapes.

2 Combine buttermilk, 2 tablespoons hot pepper sauce and salt in medium bowl; mix well. Add chicken to brine; cover and refrigerate at least 4 hours or overnight. Combine mayonnaise, remaining 1 tablespoon hot pepper sauce and Cajun seasoning in small bowl; cover and refrigerate until ready to serve.

3 Remove chicken from refrigerator 30 minutes before cooking. Heat 3 inches of oil in large saucepan over medium-high heat to 350°F; adjust heat to maintain temperature. Meanwhile, combine flour, cornstarch, paprika, black pepper, msg and red pepper in shallow dish; mix well. Drizzle 4 tablespoons buttermilk brine into flour mixture; stir with fork or fingers until mixture resembles wet sand.

4 Working with one piece at a time, remove chicken from brine and add to flour mixture. Turn to coat completely, pressing flour mixture into chicken to form thick coating. Lower chicken gently into hot oil; fry 6 to 8 minutes or until cooked through (165°F) and crust is golden brown and crisp, turning occasionally. Drain on paper towel-lined plate.

5 Spread about 1½ tablespoons mayonnaise mixture on cut sides of buns. Top bottom halves of buns with 3 to 4 pickle slices, chicken and top halves of buns. Serve immediately.

CURRIED CHICKEN WRAPS

Makes 4 servings

⅓ cup mayonnaise

2 tablespoons mango chutney

½ teaspoon curry powder

4 (6-inch) corn tortillas

1½ cups shredded coleslaw mix

1½ cups shredded cooked chicken

2 tablespoons chopped lightly salted peanuts

1 tablespoon chopped fresh cilantro, plus additional for garnish

1 Combine mayonnaise, chutney and curry powder in small bowl; mix well. Spread evenly onto one side of each tortilla.

2 Top evenly with coleslaw mix, chicken, peanuts and 1 tablespoon cilantro. Roll up to enclose filling. Cut in half diagonally to serve. Garnish with additional cilantro.

SUN-DRIED TOMATO WRAPS WITH FRIED CHICKEN

Makes 4 servings

½ cup ranch salad dressing

4 large sun-dried tomato flour tortillas, warmed, if desired

3 cups shredded lettuce

4 ounces sliced Monterey Jack cheese with hot peppers

1 can (2½ ounces) sliced black olives, drained

4 to 8 fried chicken tenders (about 1 pound), cut in half lengthwise

Hot pepper sauce (optional)

1 Spoon 2 tablespoons dressing down center of each tortilla.

2 Top with equal amounts lettuce, cheese, olives and chicken. Sprinkle lightly with hot pepper sauce, if desired. Roll tightly, folding bottom; secure with toothpicks, if necessary.

Curried
Chicken Wraps

CHICKEN PARMESAN SLIDERS

Makes 12 sliders

4 boneless skinless chicken breasts (6 to 8 ounces each)

¼ cup all-purpose flour

2 eggs

1 tablespoon water

1 cup Italian-seasoned dry bread crumbs

½ cup grated Parmesan cheese

Salt and black pepper

Olive oil

12 buns (about 3 inches), split

¾ cup marinara sauce

6 tablespoons Alfredo sauce

6 slices mozzarella cheese, cut into halves

2 tablespoons butter, melted

¼ teaspoon garlic powder

6 tablespoons pesto

1 Preheat oven to 375°F. Line baking sheet with foil; top with wire rack.

2 Pound chicken to ½-inch thickness between two sheets of waxed paper or plastic wrap with rolling pin or meat mallet. Cut each chicken breast crosswise into three pieces about the size of buns.

3 Place flour in shallow dish. Beat eggs and water in second shallow dish. Combine bread crumbs and Parmesan in third shallow dish. Season flour and egg mixtures with pinch of salt and pepper. Coat chicken pieces lightly with flour, shaking off excess. Dip in egg mixture, coating completely; roll in bread crumb mixture to coat. Place on large plate; let stand 10 minutes.

4 Heat ¼ inch oil in large nonstick skillet over medium-high heat. Add chicken in single layer (cook in two batches if necessary); cook 3 to 4 minutes per side or until golden brown. Remove chicken to wire rack; bake 5 minutes or until cooked through (165°F). Remove rack with chicken from baking sheet.

5 Arrange slider buns on foil-lined baking sheet with bottoms cut sides up and tops cut sides down. Spread 1 tablespoon marinara sauce over each bottom bun; top with piece of chicken. Spread ½ tablespoon Alfredo sauce over chicken; top with half slice of mozzarella. Combine butter and garlic powder in small bowl; brush mixture over top buns.

6 Bake 3 to 4 minutes or until mozzarella is melted and top buns are lightly toasted. Spread ½ tablespoon pesto over mozzarella; cover with top buns.

GRILLED BUFFALO CHICKEN WRAPS

Makes 4 servings

4 boneless skinless chicken breasts (about 4 ounces each)

¼ cup plus 2 tablespoons buffalo wing sauce, divided

2 cups broccoli slaw mix

1 tablespoon blue cheese salad dressing

4 (8-inch) whole wheat tortillas, warmed

1 Place chicken in large resealable food storage bag. Add ¼ cup buffalo sauce; seal bag. Marinate in refrigerator 15 minutes.

2 Meanwhile, prepare grill for direct cooking over medium-high heat. Grill chicken 5 to 6 minutes per side or until no longer pink. When cool enough to handle, slice chicken and combine with remaining 2 tablespoons buffalo sauce in medium bowl.

3 Combine broccoli slaw and blue cheese dressing in medium bowl; mix well.

4 Arrange chicken and broccoli slaw evenly down center of each tortilla. Roll up to secure filling. To serve, cut in half diagonally.

TIP: If you don't like the spicy flavor of buffalo wing sauce, substitute your favorite barbecue sauce.

CRISPY CHICKEN SANDWICH

Makes 4 servings

2 boneless skinless chicken breasts (6 to 8 ounces each)

4 cups cold water

¼ cup granulated sugar

3 tablespoons plus 1 teaspoon salt, divided

Peanut or vegetable oil for frying

1 cup milk

2 eggs

1½ cups all-purpose flour

2 tablespoons powdered sugar

2 teaspoons paprika

2 teaspoons black pepper

¾ teaspoon baking powder

½ teaspoon ground red pepper

8 dill pickle slices

4 soft hamburger buns, toasted and buttered

1 Pound chicken to ½-inch thickness between two sheets of waxed paper or plastic wrap with rolling pin or meat mallet. Cut each breast in half crosswise to create total of four pieces.

2 Combine water, granulated sugar and 3 tablespoons salt in medium bowl; stir until sugar and salt are dissolved. Add chicken to brine; cover and refrigerate 2 to 4 hours. Remove chicken from refrigerator about 30 minutes before cooking.

3 Heat at least 3 inches of oil in large saucepan over medium-high heat to 350°F; adjust heat to maintain temperature. Meanwhile, beat milk and eggs in medium shallow dish until blended. Combine flour, powdered sugar, paprika, black pepper, remaining 1 teaspoon salt, baking powder and red pepper in another shallow dish; mix well.

4 Working with one piece at a time, remove chicken from brine and add to milk mixture, turning to coat. Place in flour mixture; turn to coat completely and shake off excess. Lower chicken gently into hot oil; fry 6 to 8 minutes or until cooked through (165°F) and crust is golden brown and crisp, turning occasionally. Drain on paper towel-lined plate.

5 Place 2 pickle slices on bottom halves of buns; top with chicken and top halves of buns. Serve immediately.

CHICKEN SALAD MELT

Makes 4 servings

4 English muffins, split

2 cans (4.5 ounces **each**) SWANSON® Premium White Chunk Chicken Breast in Water, drained

1 stalk celery, finely chopped (about ½ cup)

3 tablespoons reduced fat or fat free mayonnaise

8 tomato slices

2 ounces shredded Cheddar cheese (about ½ cup)

1 Heat the oven to 400°F. Bake the muffin halves on a baking sheet for 10 minutes or until they're lightly toasted.

2 Stir the chicken, celery and mayonnaise in a small bowl.

3 Divide the chicken mixture among the muffin halves. Top with the tomato slices and cheese.

4 Bake for 10 minutes or until the cheese is melted.

CHICKEN BURGERS WITH WHITE CHEDDAR

Makes 4 servings

1¼ pounds ground chicken

1 cup plain dry bread crumbs

½ cup diced red bell pepper

½ cup ground walnuts

¼ cup sliced green onions

¼ cup light beer

2 tablespoons chopped fresh parsley

2 tablespoons lemon juice

2 cloves garlic, minced

¾ teaspoon salt

⅛ teaspoon black pepper

4 slices white Cheddar cheese

4 whole wheat buns

Dijon mustard and lettuce leaves

1 Combine chicken, bread crumbs, bell pepper, walnuts, green onions, beer, parsley, lemon juice, garlic, salt and black pepper in large bowl; mix lightly. Shape into four patties.

2 Spray large skillet with nonstick cooking spray; heat over medium-high heat. Cook patties 6 to 7 minutes on each side or until cooked through (165°F). Place cheese on patties; cover skillet just until cheese melts.

3 Serve burgers on buns with mustard and lettuce.

CHICKEN TACO SALAD WRAPS

Makes 4 servings

1 ripe large avocado, pitted, peeled and diced

¾ cup peeled and diced jicama

2 teaspoons lime juice

2 tablespoons vegetable oil

1 pound boneless skinless chicken breasts, cut into strips

1 packet (1.25 ounces) ORTEGA® Taco Seasoning Mix

¾ cup water

8 ORTEGA® Taco Shells, any variety, coarsely crushed

12 large Bibb lettuce leaves

½ cup (2 ounces) shredded Mexican cheese blend

¼ cup chopped fresh cilantro

1 jar (8 ounces) ORTEGA® Taco Sauce, any variety

COMBINE avocado, jicama and lime juice in small bowl; stir well. Set aside.

HEAT oil in large skillet over medium-high heat. Add chicken strips; cook and stir 4 to 6 minutes or until chicken is no longer pink.

STIR in seasoning mix and water. Bring to a boil. Reduce heat to low; cook 2 to 3 minutes or until mixture is thickened, stirring occasionally. Remove from heat.

MICROWAVE crushed taco shells on HIGH (100% power) 1 minute.

SPOON ⅓ cup chicken filling onto each lettuce leaf; layer with taco shells, avocado mixture, cheese and cilantro. Wrap lettuce around filling and serve with taco sauce.

CHICKEN MOZZARELLA SANDWICHES

Makes 4 servings

1 loaf (11.75 ounces) PEPPERIDGE FARM® Mozzarella Garlic Bread

2 teaspoons vegetable oil

2 skinless, boneless chicken breast halves (about ½ pound), cut into strips

½ cup PREGO® Traditional Italian Sauce

1 Prepare the bread according to the package directions.

2 Heat the oil in a 10-inch skillet over medium-high heat. Add the chicken and cook until it's well browned, stirring often.

3 Stir the Italian sauce in the skillet and heat to a boil. Reduce the heat to low. Cook until the chicken is cooked through, stirring occasionally.

4 Spoon the chicken mixture onto the bottom bread half. Top with the remaining bread half. Cut the sandwich into quarters.

COMFORTING CASSEROLES

CHICKEN ENCHILADA CASSEROLE

Makes 8 servings

- 1 teaspoon olive oil
- 1 cup chopped red onion
- 1 can (4 ounces) diced mild green chiles
- 2 cans (10 ounces each) mild enchilada sauce
- 12 ounces shredded cooked chicken breast
- ⅔ cup sliced green onions
- 12 (6-inch) corn tortillas
- ¾ cup (3 ounces) shredded Mexican cheese blend
- ½ cup sour cream (optional)

1 Preheat oven to 350°F. Heat oil in large nonstick skillet over medium-high heat. Add red onion and chiles; cook and stir 4 to 5 minutes or until red onion is tender. Add sauce, chicken and green onions.

2 Spray 2½-quart oval casserole dish with nonstick cooking spray. Place 4 tortillas in bottom of dish. Spoon 2 cups chicken mixture over tortillas; top with ¼ cup cheese. Top with 4 tortillas, 1 cup chicken mixture and ¼ cup cheese. Repeat with remaining 4 tortillas, chicken mixture and cheese.

3 Cover and bake 20 minutes. Remove cover and bake an additional 10 minutes or until thoroughly heated. Let stand 10 minutes before serving. Serve with sour cream, if desired.

ARTICHOKE-OLIVE CHICKEN BAKE

Makes 8 servings

1½ cups uncooked rotini pasta

1 tablespoon olive oil

1 medium onion, chopped

½ green bell pepper, chopped

2 cups shredded cooked chicken

1 can (about 14 ounces) diced tomatoes with Italian seasoning

1 can (14 ounces) artichoke hearts, drained and quartered

1 can (6 ounces) sliced black olives, drained

1 teaspoon Italian seasoning

2 cups (8 ounces) shredded mozzarella cheese

1 Preheat oven to 350°F. Spray 2-quart casserole with nonstick cooking spray. Cook pasta according to package directions; drain.

2 Heat oil in large skillet over medium heat. Add onion and bell pepper; cook and stir 1 minute. Add pasta, chicken, tomatoes, artichokes, olives and Italian seasoning; mix until blended.

3 Place half of chicken mixture in prepared casserole; sprinkle with half of cheese. Top with remaining chicken mixture and cheese.

4 Bake, covered, 35 minutes or until hot and bubbly.

MEDITERRANEAN MAC & CHEESE

Makes 4 to 6 servings

8 ounces uncooked elbow macaroni or other small pasta shape

1 tablespoon olive oil

1 red bell pepper, cut into slivers

1 bunch (about ¾ pound) asparagus, cut into 1-inch pieces

4 tablespoons (½ stick) butter, divided

¼ cup all-purpose flour

1¾ cups milk, heated

1 teaspoon minced fresh thyme

Salt and black pepper

1 cup (4 ounces) shredded mozzarella cheese

1 cup (1-inch pieces) cooked chicken

4 ounces garlic and herb flavored goat cheese

¼ cup plain dry bread crumbs

1 Preheat oven to 350°F. Cook macaroni according to package directions until almost al dente. Rinse under cold running water to stop the cooking process; set aside.

2 Meanwhile, heat oil in medium skillet over medium-high heat; cook and stir bell pepper 3 minutes. Add asparagus; cook and stir 3 minutes or until crisp-tender. Remove from skillet.

3 Melt 3 tablespoons butter over medium-low heat in large saucepan or deep skillet until bubbly. Whisk in flour until smooth paste forms; cook and stir 2 minutes without browning. Gradually whisk in milk. Turn heat to medium; cook 6 to 8 minutes, whisking constantly until mixture begins to bubble and thickens slightly. Add thyme and season with salt and black pepper. Remove from heat.

4 Stir in mozzarella cheese until melted. Add pasta, bell pepper, asparagus and chicken to cheese sauce. Crumble goat cheese into mixture; remove to 2-quart casserole. Top with bread crumbs and dot with remaining 1 tablespoon butter.

5 Bake 25 to 30 minutes or until lightly browned and bubbly.

BAKED ITALIAN CHICKEN & PASTA

Makes 4 servings

1 can (10¾ ounces) CAMPBELL'S® Condensed Tomato Soup

1⅓ cups water

1 teaspoon dried basil leaves, crushed

2 cups **uncooked** corkscrew-shaped pasta (rotini)

4 skinless, boneless chicken breast halves (about 1 pound)

½ cup shredded mozzarella cheese

1 Stir the soup, water, basil and pasta in a 2-quart shallow baking dish. Top with the chicken. Sprinkle with the cheese and additional basil, if desired. Cover the baking dish.

2 Bake at 350°F. for 45 minutes or until the chicken is cooked through and the pasta is tender.

CHICKEN & BISCUITS

Makes 4 to 6 servings

¼ cup (½ stick) butter

4 boneless skinless chicken breasts (about 1¼ pounds), cut into ½-inch pieces

½ cup chopped onion

Salt and black pepper

1 can (about 14 ounces) chicken broth, divided

⅓ cup all-purpose flour

1 package (10 ounces) frozen peas and carrots

1 can (12 ounces) refrigerated buttermilk biscuits

1 Preheat oven to 375°F. Melt butter in large skillet over medium heat. Add chicken, onion, salt and pepper; cook and stir 5 minutes or until chicken is browned.

2 Combine ¼ cup broth and flour in small bowl; stir until smooth. Add remaining broth to skillet; bring to a boil. Gradually add flour mixture, whisking constantly to prevent lumps from forming. Simmer 5 minutes. Add peas and carrots; cook 2 minutes. Remove mixture to 1½-quart casserole; top with biscuits. Bake 25 to 30 minutes or until biscuits are golden brown.

Baked Italian
Chicken & Pasta

CREAMY CHICKEN ENCHILADAS

Makes 6 servings

1 can (10¾ ounces) CAMPBELL'S® Condensed Cream of Chicken Soup (Regular or 98% Fat Free)

1 container (8 ounces) sour cream

1 cup PACE® Picante Sauce

2 teaspoons chili powder

2 cups chopped cooked chicken

1 cup shredded Monterey Jack cheese (4 ounces)

12 flour tortillas (8-inch), warmed

1 medium tomato, chopped (about 1 cup)

1 green onion, sliced (about 2 tablespoons)

1 Mix the soup, sour cream, picante sauce and chili powder in a small bowl.

2 Stir **1 cup** of the soup mixture, chicken and cheese in a medium bowl.

3 Spoon about ¼ **cup** of the chicken mixture down the center of each tortilla. Roll up the tortillas and place them seam-side down in 13×9-inch (3-quart) shallow baking dish. Pour the remaining soup mixture over the filled tortillas. **Cover.**

4 Bake at 350°F. for 40 minutes or until hot and bubbly. Top with the tomato and green onion.

KITCHEN TIP: For **2 cups** chopped cooked chicken, in medium saucepan over medium heat, in **4 cups** boiling water, cook **1 pound** skinless, boneless chicken breasts or thighs, cubed, 5 minutes or until chicken is no longer pink. Drain and chop chicken.

PENNE CHICKEN CASSEROLE

Makes 6 servings

1½ pounds boneless skinless chicken breasts

3 cups water

2 cubes beef bouillon

4 cups cooked penne pasta

1 can (10¾ ounces) condensed cream of chicken soup, undiluted

1 cup sour cream

½ cup grated Asiago cheese

½ cup mayonnaise

⅓ cup dry sherry

½ cup dry Italian-seasoned bread crumbs

¼ cup grated Parmesan cheese

¼ cup (½ stick) butter, melted

1 Preheat oven to 350°F. Spray 2-quart casserole with nonstick cooking spray. Place chicken, water and bouillon cubes in large saucepan over medium heat. Cook 20 minutes or until chicken is no longer pink in center. Drain liquid and discard; cut chicken into cubes. Combine pasta and chicken in prepared casserole.

2 Combine soup, sour cream, Asiago cheese, mayonnaise and sherry in medium bowl; mix well. Spoon evenly over pasta and chicken.

3 Toss bread crumbs, Parmesan cheese and butter in small bowl. Sprinkle over casserole. Bake 30 to 45 minutes or until top is golden brown.

WILD RICE & CHICKEN CASSEROLE

Makes 4 to 6 servings

1 package (6 ounces) long grain & wild rice mix

2 tablespoons butter

½ cup chopped onion

½ cup chopped celery

2 cups cubed cooked chicken

1 can (10¾ ounces) condensed cream of mushroom soup, undiluted

½ cup sour cream

⅓ cup dry white wine

½ teaspoon curry powder

1 Preheat oven to 350°F.

2 Prepare rice mix according to package directions.

3 Meanwhile, melt butter in large skillet over medium heat. Add onion and celery; cook and stir 5 to 7 minutes until tender. Stir in rice, chicken, soup, sour cream, wine and curry powder. Remove rice mixture to 2-quart casserole.

4 Bake 40 minutes or until heated through.

CHICKEN CASSOULET

Makes 6 servings

4 slices bacon

¼ cup all-purpose flour

Salt and black pepper

1¾ pounds bone-in chicken pieces

2 chicken sausages (2¼ ounces each), cooked and cut into ¼-inch pieces

1 medium onion, chopped

1½ cups diced red and green bell peppers

2 cloves garlic, minced

1 teaspoon dried thyme

1 teaspoon olive oil

½ cup dry white wine

2 cans (about 15 ounces each) cannellini or Great Northern beans, rinsed and drained

1 Preheat oven to 350°F.

2 Cook bacon in Dutch oven over medium-high heat until crisp; drain on paper towels. Cut into 1-inch pieces. Reserve bacon drippings in Dutch oven.

3 Place flour in shallow bowl; season with salt and black pepper. Dip chicken pieces in flour mixture; shake off excess. Brown chicken in batches in Dutch oven with bacon drippings over medium-high heat; remove to plate. Lightly brown sausages in same Dutch oven; remove to plate.

4 Add onion, bell peppers, garlic and thyme to Dutch oven; cook and stir over medium heat 5 minutes or until softened, adding oil as needed to prevent sticking. Add wine; cook and stir over medium heat, scraping up browned bits from bottom of pan. Add beans; mix well. Top with chicken, sausages and bacon.

5 Cover and bake 40 minutes. Uncover; bake 15 minutes or until chicken is cooked through (165°F).

CHICKEN ZUCCHINI CASSEROLE

Makes 8 servings

1 package (about 6 ounces) herb-flavored stuffing mix

½ cup (1 stick) butter, melted

2 cups cubed zucchini

1½ cups chopped cooked chicken

1 can (10¾ ounces) condensed cream of celery soup, undiluted

1 cup grated carrots

1 onion, chopped

½ cup sour cream

½ cup (2 ounces) shredded Cheddar cheese

1 Preheat oven to 350°F. Combine stuffing mix and butter in medium bowl; reserve 1 cup stuffing. Place remaining stuffing in 13×9-inch baking dish.

2 Combine zucchini, chicken, soup, carrots, onion and sour cream in large bowl; mix well. Pour over stuffing in baking dish; top with reserved 1 cup stuffing and cheese.

3 Bake 40 to 45 minutes or until heated through and cheese is melted.

APPLE CURRY CHICKEN

Makes 4 servings

- 4 boneless skinless chicken breasts
- 1 cup apple juice, divided
- ¼ teaspoon salt
- Dash black pepper
- 1½ cups plain croutons
- 1 green apple, chopped

- 1 onion, chopped
- ¼ cup raisins
- 2 teaspoons packed brown sugar
- 1 teaspoon curry powder
- ¾ teaspoon poultry seasoning
- ⅛ teaspoon garlic powder

1 Preheat oven to 350°F. Lightly coat 2-quart baking dish with nonstick cooking spray.

2 Arrange chicken in single layer in prepared baking dish. Combine ¼ cup apple juice, salt and pepper in small bowl. Brush juice mixture over chicken.

3 Combine croutons, apple, onion, raisins, brown sugar, curry powder, poultry seasoning and garlic powder in large bowl. Toss with remaining ¾ cup apple juice.

4 Spoon crouton mixture over chicken. Cover with foil; bake 45 minutes or until chicken is no longer pink in center.

CHICKEN NOODLE CASSEROLE

Makes 4 to 6 servings

1 package (12 ounces) uncooked wide egg noodles

2 cups chopped cooked chicken

1 can (10¾ ounces) condensed cream of mushroom soup, undiluted

1 cup (4 ounces) shredded Cheddar-Jack cheese

½ cup sour cream

½ cup milk

⅓ to ½ cup plain dry bread crumbs

1 to 2 tablespoons chopped fresh parsley (optional)

1 Preheat oven to 350°F. Spray 13×9-inch baking pan with nonstick cooking spray.

2 Cook noodles according to package directions; drain. Return to saucepan. Add chicken, soup, cheese, sour cream and milk; mix well. Remove to prepared pan; top with bread crumbs.

3 Bake 25 minutes or until hot and bubbly. Garnish with parsley.

CHICKEN-ASPARAGUS CASSEROLE

Makes 12 servings

2 teaspoons vegetable oil

1 cup chopped green and/or red bell peppers

1 medium onion, chopped

2 cloves garlic, minced

1 can (10¾ ounces) condensed cream of asparagus soup, undiluted

1 container (8 ounces) ricotta cheese

2 cups (8 ounces) shredded Cheddar cheese, divided

2 eggs

1½ cups chopped cooked chicken

1 package (10 ounces) frozen chopped asparagus,* thawed and drained

8 ounces egg noodles, cooked and drained

Salt and black pepper (optional)

*Or substitute ½ pound fresh asparagus cut into ½-inch pieces. Bring 6 cups water to a boil in large saucepan over high heat. Add asparagus; cover and cook over medium heat 5 to 8 minutes or until crisp-tender. Drain.

1 Preheat oven to 350°F. Spray 13×9-inch baking dish with nonstick cooking spray.

2 Heat oil in medium skillet over medium heat. Add bell peppers, onion and garlic; cook and stir until vegetables are crisp-tender.

3 Mix soup, ricotta cheese, 1 cup Cheddar cheese and eggs in large bowl until well blended. Add onion mixture, chicken, asparagus and noodles; mix well. Season with salt and black pepper, if desired. Spread mixture in prepared baking dish; sprinkle with remaining 1 cup Cheddar cheese.

4 Bake 30 minutes or until center is set and cheese is bubbly. Let stand 5 minutes before serving.

CHICKEN POT PIE

Makes 4 to 6 servings

1¼ cups all-purpose baking mix, divided

1 can (about 14 ounces) chicken broth

¾ cup milk

⅓ cup plus 2 tablespoons butter, divided

½ cup chopped onion

1 teaspoon minced garlic

¼ teaspoon dried rosemary

¼ teaspoon black pepper

1 package (16 ounces) frozen mixed vegetables, thawed

2 cups chopped cooked chicken

¼ cup water

1 Preheat oven to 425°F. Combine ¼ cup baking mix, broth and milk in small bowl; set aside.

2 Melt 2 tablespoons butter in large saucepan over medium heat. Add onion, garlic, rosemary and pepper; cook and stir 3 to 4 minutes or until onion is translucent. Stir broth mixture; add to onion mixture, stirring constantly until smooth. Bring to a boil; stir in vegetables and chicken. Reduce heat to medium; cook until thickened, stirring occasionally. Remove from heat; keep warm.

3 Combine remaining 1 cup baking mix, ⅓ cup butter and water in medium bowl until blended. Pat dough out into ½-inch-thick disc on waxed paper to fit top of 2-quart baking dish. Remove chicken mixture to baking dish; place crust over filling. Make several slits in crust to allow steam to escape.

4 Bake 20 minutes or until crust is browned and filling is bubbly.

VARIATION: If you like a thicker crust on your pot pie, simply double the amounts for the dough.

ZUCCHINI, CHICKEN & RICE CASSEROLE

Makes 4 servings

Vegetable cooking spray

1 package (12 ounces) refrigerated **or** thawed frozen breaded cooked chicken tenders, cut into bite-sized strips

2 large zucchini, cut in half lengthwise and thinly sliced (about 4 cups)

1 jar (7 ounces) whole roasted sweet peppers, drained and thinly sliced

1 cup **uncooked** quick-cooking brown rice

1 can (10¾ ounces) CAMPBELL'S® Condensed Cream of Celery Soup (Regular **or** 98% Fat Free)

1 soup can water

½ cup sour cream

1 Heat the oven to 375°F. Spray a 3-quart shallow baking dish with the cooking spray.

2 Stir the chicken, zucchini, peppers and rice in the baking dish.

3 Stir the soup, water and sour cream in a small bowl. Pour the soup mixture over the chicken mixture. Cover the baking dish.

4 Bake for 35 minutes or until the rice is tender. Let stand for 10 minutes. Stir the rice before serving.

KITCHEN TIP: Choose zucchini that have firm, dark green skin.

CHICKEN TETRAZZINI

Makes 6 servings

8 ounces uncooked vermicelli or other thin noodle

2 teaspoons butter

8 ounces mushrooms, sliced

¼ cup chopped green onions

1 can (about 14 ounces) chicken broth

1 cup milk, divided

2 tablespoons dry sherry

¼ cup all-purpose flour

¼ teaspoon salt

¼ teaspoon ground nutmeg

⅛ teaspoon white pepper

2 ounces chopped pimientos, drained

4 tablespoons grated Parmesan cheese, divided

½ cup sour cream

2 cups cooked boneless skinless chicken breasts, cut into 1-inch pieces

1 Preheat oven to 350°F. Lightly coat 1½-quart casserole with nonstick cooking spray. Cook noodles according to package directions, omitting salt. Drain; set aside.

2 Melt butter in large nonstick skillet over medium-high heat. Add mushrooms and green onions; cook and stir 8 minutes or until onions are tender. Add broth, ½ cup milk and sherry to onion mixture. Pour remaining ½ cup milk into small jar with tight-fitting lid; add flour, salt, nutmeg and pepper. Shake well. Slowly stir flour mixture into skillet. Bring to a boil; cook 1 minute. Reduce heat to low; stir in pimientos and 2 tablespoons Parmesan cheese. Stir in sour cream; blend well. Add chicken and noodles; mix well.

3 Spread mixture evenly into prepared casserole. Sprinkle with remaining 2 tablespoons Parmesan cheese. Bake 30 to 35 minutes or until heated through. Let cool slightly. Cut into six wedges before serving.

SOUPS AND SALADS

MEDITERRANEAN SALAD

Makes 4 servings

- 2 cups chopped iceberg lettuce
- 2 cups baby spinach
- 2 cups diced cucumbers
- 1 cup diced cooked chicken
- 1 cup chopped roasted red peppers

- 1 cup grape tomatoes, halved
- 1 cup quartered artichoke hearts
- ¾ cup crumbled feta cheese
- ½ cup chopped red onion
- 1 cup hummus
- ½ teaspoon Italian seasoning

1 Divide lettuce and spinach among four salad bowls or plates; top with cucumbers, chicken, roasted peppers, tomatoes, artichokes, cheese and onion.

2 Top salad with hummus; sprinkle with Italian seasoning.

CREAM OF CHICKEN AND TORTELLINI SOUP

Makes 4 servings

½ of an 8-ounce package dried tortellini with mushrooms and chicken

2 tablespoons butter

1 cup fresh snow peas, cut into 1-inch pieces

2 tablespoons all-purpose flour

3 cups chicken broth, heated

¼ cup half-and-half

1 cup diced cooked chicken breast

1 green onion, chopped

¼ cup grated Parmesan cheese (optional)

1 Cook tortellini according to package directions or until tender. Drain and set aside.

2 Meanwhile, melt butter in large saucepan over medium heat. Add snow peas; cook and stir 3 minutes or until crisp-tender. Stir in flour; cook and stir 1 minute. Stir in broth; cook and stir until mixture is slightly thickened. Stir in half-and-half, chicken, green onion and tortellini. Simmer 2 minutes or until pasta is heated through.

3 Garnish with cheese.

COBB SALAD
Makes 4 servings

1 package (10 ounces) torn mixed salad greens *or* 8 cups torn romaine lettuce

6 ounces deli chicken, diced

1 large tomato, seeded and chopped

⅓ cup bacon, crisp-cooked and crumbled or bacon bits

1 large ripe avocado, diced

Crumbled blue cheese

Prepared blue cheese or Caesar salad dressing

French or Italian rolls (optional)

1 Place salad greens in serving bowl. Arrange chicken, tomato, bacon and avocado in rows.

2 Sprinkle with blue cheese. Serve with dressing and bread, if desired.

CRUNCHY RAMEN CHICKEN SALAD
Makes 4 servings

2 cups chopped cooked chicken (about 4 ounces)

1 package (8 ounces) broccoli slaw mix or coleslaw mix

1 can (11 ounces) mandarin oranges in light syrup, drained

¼ cup coleslaw dressing

1 package (3 ounces) ramen noodles, any flavor, crumbled*

*Discard seasoning packet.

1 Combine chicken, broccoli slaw, oranges and dressing in medium bowl; stir to blend. Cover; refrigerate until ready to serve.

2 Just before serving, add crumbled noodles. Stir to combine.

Cobb Salad

SPICY SQUASH AND CHICKEN SOUP

Makes 4 servings

1 tablespoon vegetable oil

1 small onion, finely chopped

1 stalk celery, finely chopped

2 cups cubed delicata or butternut squash (about 1 small)

2 cups chicken broth

1 can (about 14 ounces) diced tomatoes with green chiles

1 cup chopped cooked chicken

½ teaspoon ground ginger

¼ teaspoon salt

⅛ teaspoon ground cumin

⅛ teaspoon black pepper

2 teaspoons lime juice

Sprigs fresh parsley or cilantro (optional)

1 Heat oil in large saucepan over medium heat. Add onion and celery; cook and stir 5 minutes or just until vegetables are tender. Stir in squash, broth, tomatoes, chicken, ginger, salt, cumin and pepper; bring to a boil.

2 Reduce heat to low; cover and cook 30 minutes or until squash is tender. Stir in lime juice. Sprinkle with parsley, if desired.

TIP: Delicata and butternut are two types of winter squash. Delicata is an elongated, creamy yellow squash with green striations. Butternut is a long, light orange squash. Both have hard skins. To use, cut the squash lengthwise, scoop out the seeds, peel and cut into cubes.

THAI COCONUT CHICKEN AND RICE SOUP

Makes 6 to 8 servings

1 pound boneless skinless chicken thighs, cut into 1-inch pieces

3 cups chicken broth

1 package (12 ounces) frozen chopped onions

1 can (4 ounces) sliced mushrooms, drained

2 tablespoons minced fresh ginger

2 tablespoons sugar

1 cup cooked rice

1 can (15 ounces) unsweetened coconut milk

½ red bell pepper, seeded and thinly sliced

3 tablespoons chopped fresh cilantro

2 tablespoons grated lime peel

Slow Cooker Directions

1 Combine chicken, broth, onions, mushrooms, ginger and sugar in slow cooker; stir to blend. Cover; cook on LOW 8 to 9 hours.

2 Stir rice, coconut milk and bell pepper into soup. Cover; cook on LOW 15 minutes. Turn off heat. Stir in cilantro and lime peel.

TIP: One medium lime will yield about 1½ teaspoons grated lime peel. You will need about 4 medium limes to get 2 tablespoons grated lime peel.

CHICKEN CAESAR SALAD

Makes 4 servings

4 small boneless skinless chicken breasts

6 ounces uncooked gnocchi or other dried pasta

1 package (9 ounces) frozen artichoke hearts, thawed

1½ cups cherry tomatoes, quartered

¼ cup plus 2 tablespoons plain nonfat yogurt

2 tablespoons mayonnaise

2 tablespoons grated Romano cheese

1 tablespoon sherry or red wine vinegar

1 clove garlic, minced

½ teaspoon anchovy paste

½ teaspoon Dijon mustard

½ teaspoon white pepper

1 small head romaine lettuce, torn into bite-size pieces

1 cup toasted bread cubes

1 Grill or broil chicken breasts 6 to 8 minutes or until no longer pink in center; set aside.

2 Cook pasta according to package directions. Drain and rinse well under cold running water until pasta is cool; drain well. Combine pasta, artichoke hearts and tomatoes in large bowl; set aside.

3 Combine yogurt, mayonnaise, Romano cheese, sherry, garlic, anchovy paste, mustard and pepper in small bowl; whisk until smooth. Add to pasta mixture; toss to coat evenly.

4 Arrange lettuce on platter or individual plates. Spoon pasta mixture over lettuce. Thinly slice chicken breasts and place on top of pasta. Sprinkle with bread cubes.

CHICKEN NOODLE SOUP

Makes 8 servings

- 2 tablespoons butter
- 1 cup chopped onion
- 1 cup sliced carrots
- ½ cup diced celery
- 2 tablespoons vegetable oil
- 1 pound chicken breast tenderloins
- 1 pound chicken thigh fillets

- 4 cups chicken broth, divided
- 2 cups water
- 1 tablespoon minced fresh parsley, plus additional for garnish
- 1½ teaspoons salt
- ½ teaspoon black pepper
- 3 cups uncooked egg noodles

1 Melt butter in large saucepan or Dutch oven over medium-low heat. Add onion, carrots and celery; cook 8 minutes or until vegetables are soft, stirring occasionally.

2 Meanwhile, heat oil in large skillet over medium-high heat. Add chicken in single layer; cook 12 minutes or until lightly browned and cooked through, turning once. Remove chicken to large cutting board. Add 1 cup broth to skillet; cook 1 minute, scraping up browned bits from bottom of skillet. Add broth to vegetables in saucepan. Stir in remaining 3 cups broth, water, 1 tablespoon parsley, salt and pepper.

3 Chop chicken into 1-inch pieces when cool enough to handle. Add to soup; bring to a boil over medium-high heat. Reduce heat to medium-low; cook 15 minutes. Add noodles; cook 15 minutes or until noodles are tender. Ladle into bowls; garnish with additional parsley.

BBQ CHICKEN SALAD

Makes 4 servings

Dressing

- ¾ cup mayonnaise
- ⅓ cup buttermilk
- ¼ cup sour cream
- 1 tablespoon white wine vinegar
- 1 teaspoon sugar
- ¼ teaspoon salt
- ¼ teaspoon garlic powder
- ¼ teaspoon onion powder
- ¼ teaspoon dried parsley flakes
- ¼ teaspoon dried dill weed
- ¼ teaspoon black pepper

Salad

- 12 to 16 ounces grilled chicken breast strips
- ½ cup barbecue sauce
- 4 cups chopped romaine lettuce
- 4 cups chopped iceberg lettuce
- 2 medium tomatoes, seeded and chopped
- ¾ cup canned or thawed frozen corn, drained
- ¾ cup diced jicama
- ¾ cup (3 ounces) shredded Monterey Jack cheese
- ¼ cup chopped fresh cilantro
- 2 green onions, sliced
- 1 cup crispy tortilla strips*

*If tortilla strips are unavailable, crumble regular tortilla chips.

1 For dressing, whisk mayonnaise, buttermilk, sour cream, vinegar, sugar, salt, garlic powder, onion powder, parsley flakes, dill weed and pepper in medium bowl until well blended. Cover and refrigerate until ready to serve.

2 For salad, cut chicken strips into ½-inch pieces. Combine chicken and barbecue sauce in medium bowl; toss to coat.

3 Combine lettuce, tomatoes, corn, jicama, cheese and cilantro in large bowl. Add two thirds of dressing; toss to coat. Add remaining dressing, if necessary. Divide salad among four plates; top with chicken, green onions and tortilla strips.

ALMOND CHICKEN SALAD SANDWICH

Makes 4 servings

¼ cup mayonnaise

¼ cup plain Greek yogurt
    or sour cream

2 tablespoons cider vinegar

1 tablespoon honey

1 teaspoon salt

½ teaspoon black pepper

⅛ teaspoon garlic powder

2 cups chopped cooked chicken

¾ cup halved red grapes

1 large stalk celery, chopped

⅓ cup sliced almonds

  Leaf lettuce

1 tomato, thinly sliced

8 slices sesame semolina or
    country Italian bread

1 Whisk mayonnaise, yogurt, vinegar, honey, salt, pepper and garlic powder in small bowl until well blended.

2 Combine chicken, grapes and celery in medium bowl. Add dressing; toss gently to coat. Cover and refrigerate several hours or overnight. Stir in almonds just before making sandwiches.

3 Place lettuce and tomato slices on 4 bread slices; top with chicken salad and remaining bread slices. Serve immediately.

ONE-POT CHINESE CHICKEN SOUP

Makes 4 servings

6 cups chicken broth

2 cups water

1 pound boneless skinless chicken thighs

⅓ cup soy sauce

1 package (16 ounces) frozen stir-fry vegetables

6 ounces uncooked dried thin Chinese egg noodles

1 to 3 tablespoons sriracha sauce

1 Combine broth, water, chicken and soy sauce in medium saucepan; bring to a boil over high heat. Reduce heat to low; cover and simmer 20 minutes or until chicken is cooked through and very tender. Remove chicken to bowl; let stand until cool enough to handle.

2 Meanwhile, add vegetables and noodles to broth in saucepan; bring to a boil over high heat. Reduce heat to medium-high; cook and stir 5 minutes or until noodles are tender and vegetables are heated through.

3 Shred chicken into bite-size pieces. Stir chicken and 1 tablespoon sriracha into soup; taste and add additional sriracha for a spicier flavor.

AUTUMN HARVEST SALAD
Makes 6 servings

Dressing

- ½ cup extra virgin olive oil
- 3 tablespoons balsamic vinegar
- 1 clove garlic, minced
- 1 teaspoon honey
- 1 teaspoon Dijon mustard
- ½ teaspoon dried oregano
- ½ teaspoon salt
- ⅛ teaspoon black pepper

Salad

- 1 loaf (12 to 16 ounces) artisan pecan raisin bread
- 4 tablespoons (½ stick) butter, melted
- 6 tablespoons coarse sugar (such as demerara, turbinado or organic cane sugar)
- 6 cups packed spring greens
- 2 Granny Smith apples, thinly sliced
- 18 to 24 ounces grilled chicken breast strips
- ¾ cup crumbled blue cheese
- ¾ cup dried cranberries
- ¾ cup toasted walnuts

1 For dressing, whisk oil, vinegar, garlic, honey, mustard, oregano, salt and pepper in medium bowl until well blended. Refrigerate until ready to use.

2 Preheat oven to 350°F. Line baking sheet with parchment paper. Cut bread into thin (¼-inch) slices; place in single layer on prepared baking sheet. Brush one side of each slice with melted butter; sprinkle each slice with ½ teaspoon sugar. Bake 10 minutes. Turn slices; brush with butter and sprinkle with ½ teaspoon sugar. Bake 10 minutes. Cool completely on baking sheet.

3 For each salad, place greens on serving plate. Top evenly with apple slices, chicken strips, cheese, cranberries and walnuts. Break toast slices into pieces and sprinkle over salad. Drizzle with dressing.

CHICKEN TORTILLA AND RICE SOUP

Makes 6 servings

2 cups MINUTE® White Rice, uncooked

5 cups low-sodium chicken broth

1 cup carrots, peeled and sliced thin

1 can (10 ounces) diced tomatoes with green chiles

1 cup (6 ounces) cooked chicken breast, cubed

1 tablespoon lime juice (optional)

20 baked tortilla chips (about 1 cup), slightly crushed

½ cup low-fat Mexican cheese blend, shredded

¼ cup fresh cilantro, chopped

1 avocado, diced (optional)

PREPARE rice according to package directions.

BRING broth to a boil in medium pot. Reduce heat and add carrots, tomatoes with chiles and chicken; simmer 10 minutes.

STIR in rice; add lime juice, if desired. Divide equally into serving bowls and top with tortilla chips, cheese, cilantro and avocado, if desired.

TIP: To dice an avocado, insert a knife into the stem end. Slice in half lengthwise to the pit, turning the avocado while slicing. Twist the halves in opposite directions to pull apart. Press the knife blade into the pit, twisting gently to pull the pit away from the avocado. Discard the pit. Cut the avocado flesh in a crisscross fashion, then run a spoon underneath to scoop out the pieces.

CHICKEN WALDORF SALAD

Makes 4 servings

Dressing

- ⅓ cup balsamic vinegar
- 2 tablespoons Dijon mustard
- 2 teaspoons minced garlic
- ½ teaspoon salt
- ¼ teaspoon black pepper

- ⅔ cup extra virgin olive oil

Salad

- 8 cups mixed greens
- 1 large Granny Smith apple, cut into ½-inch pieces
- ⅔ cup diced celery
- ⅔ cup halved red seedless grapes
- 12 to 16 ounces grilled chicken breast strips
- ½ cup candied walnuts
- ½ cup crumbled blue cheese

1 For dressing, combine vinegar, mustard, garlic, salt and pepper in medium bowl; mix well. Slowly add oil, whisking until well blended.

2 For salad, combine mixed greens, apple, celery and grapes in large bowl. Add half of dressing; toss to coat. Top with chicken, walnuts and cheese; drizzle with additional dressing.

PECAN-CRUSTED CHICKEN SALAD

Makes 4 servings

Chicken

½ cup all-purpose flour

½ cup milk

1 egg

⅔ cup corn flake crumbs

⅔ cup finely chopped pecans

¾ teaspoon salt

4 boneless skinless chicken breasts (1¼ to 1½ pounds total)

Dressing

⅓ cup balsamic vinegar

1 tablespoon Dijon mustard

1 tablespoon sugar

1 teaspoon minced garlic

½ teaspoon salt

⅔ cup canola oil

Salad

10 cups mixed greens (1-pound package)

2 cans (11 ounces each) mandarin oranges, drained

1 cup sliced celery

¾ cup dried cranberries

½ cup glazed pecans*

½ cup crumbled blue cheese

*Glazed or candied pecans are often found in the produce section of the supermarket along with other salad convenience items.

1 Preheat oven to 400°F. Line baking sheet with foil; spray with nonstick cooking spray.

2 Place flour in shallow dish. Beat milk and egg in another shallow dish. Combine corn flake crumbs, chopped pecans and ¾ teaspoon salt in third shallow dish. Dip both sides of chicken in flour, then in egg mixture, letting excess drip back into dish. Roll in crumb mixture to coat completely, pressing crumbs into chicken to adhere. Place on prepared baking sheet.

3 Bake 20 minutes or until chicken is cooked through (165°F). Cool completely before slicing.

4 Meanwhile, prepare dressing. Combine vinegar, mustard, sugar, garlic and ½ teaspoon salt in medium bowl; mix well. Slowly add oil, whisking until well blended.

5 For salad, combine mixed greens, mandarin oranges, celery, cranberries, glazed pecans and cheese in large bowl. Add two thirds of dressing; toss gently to coat. Divide salad among four plates. Cut chicken breasts diagonally into ½-inch slices; arrange over salads. Serve with remaining dressing.

SUPERFOOD KALE SALAD

Makes 4 servings

Maple-Roasted Carrots

- 8 carrots, trimmed
- 2 tablespoons maple syrup
- 2 tablespoons olive oil
- ½ teaspoon salt
- ⅛ teaspoon black pepper
- Dash ground red pepper

Maple-Lemon Vinaigrette

- ¼ cup extra virgin olive oil
- 3 tablespoons lemon juice
- 2 tablespoons maple syrup
- ¾ teaspoon grated lemon peel
- ½ teaspoon salt
- ⅛ teaspoon black pepper

Salad

- 4 cups chopped kale
- 2 cups chopped mixed greens
- 1 cup dried cranberries
- 1 cup slivered almonds, toasted*
- 1 cup shredded Parmesan cheese
- 12 to 16 ounces grilled chicken breast strips

*To toast almonds, spread on ungreased baking sheet. Bake in preheated 350°F oven 6 to 8 minutes or until lightly browned, stirring occasionally.

1 Preheat oven to 400°F. Line baking sheet with parchment paper.

2 Place carrots on prepared baking sheet. Whisk 2 tablespoons maple syrup, 2 tablespoons oil, ½ teaspoon salt, ⅛ teaspoon black pepper and red pepper in small bowl until well blended. Brush some of oil mixture over carrots. Roast 30 minutes or until carrots are tender, brushing with oil mixture and shaking baking sheet every 10 minutes. Cut carrots crosswise into ¼-inch slices when cool enough to handle.

3 While carrots are roasting, prepare vinaigrette. Whisk ¼ cup oil, lemon juice, 2 tablespoons maple syrup, lemon peel, ½ teaspoon salt and ⅛ teaspoon black pepper in small bowl until well blended.

4 Combine kale, greens, cranberries, almonds and cheese in large bowl. Add carrots. Pour vinaigrette over salad; toss to coat. Top with chicken.

EASY CHICKEN, SPINACH AND WILD RICE SOUP

Makes 6 to 7 servings

1 can (about 14 ounces) chicken broth

1¾ cups chopped carrots

2 cans (10¾ ounces each) condensed cream of chicken soup, undiluted

2 cups cooked wild rice

1 teaspoon dried thyme

¼ teaspoon dried sage

¼ teaspoon black pepper

2 cups coarsely chopped baby spinach

1½ cups chopped cooked chicken*

½ cup half-and-half or milk

*Half of a rotisserie chicken will yield about 1½ cups of cooked meat.

1 Bring broth to a boil in large saucepan over medium-high heat. Add carrots; cook 10 minutes.

2 Add soup, rice, thyme, sage and pepper to saucepan; bring to a boil. Stir in spinach, chicken and half-and-half; cook and stir 2 minutes or until heated through.

CLASSIC DINNERS

CHIPOTLE SPICE-RUBBED BEER CAN CHICKEN

Makes 4 servings

- 2 tablespoons packed brown sugar
- 2 teaspoons smoked paprika
- 2 teaspoons ground cumin
- 1 teaspoon salt
- 1 teaspoon garlic powder
- 1 teaspoon chili powder
- ½ teaspoon ground chipotle pepper
- 1 whole chicken (3½ to 4 pounds), rinsed and patted dry
- 1 can (12 ounces) beer

1 Prepare grill for indirect cooking over medium heat.

2 Combine brown sugar, paprika, cumin, salt, garlic powder, chili powder and chipotle pepper in small bowl. Gently loosen skin of chicken over breast, legs and thighs. Rub sugar mixture under and over skin and inside cavity. Discard one fourth of beer. Hold chicken upright with cavity pointing down; insert beer can into cavity.

3 Oil grid. Place chicken on grid, standing upright on can. Spread legs slightly for support. Grill, covered, 1 hour 15 minutes or until chicken is cooked through (165°F).

4 Lift chicken off beer can using metal tongs. Let rest upright on cutting board 5 minutes before carving.

FORTY-CLOVE CHICKEN FILICE

Makes 4 to 6 servings

¼ cup olive oil

1 cut-up whole chicken (about 3 pounds)

40 cloves garlic (about 2 heads), peeled

4 stalks celery, thickly sliced

½ cup dry white wine

¼ cup dry vermouth

Grated peel and juice of 1 lemon

2 tablespoons finely chopped fresh parsley

2 teaspoons dried basil

1 teaspoon dried oregano, crushed

Pinch red pepper flakes

Salt and black pepper

1 Preheat oven to 375°F.

2 Heat oil in Dutch oven. Add chicken; cook until browned on all sides.

3 Combine garlic, celery, wine, vermouth, lemon juice, parsley, basil, oregano and red pepper flakes in medium bowl; pour over chicken. Sprinkle with lemon peel; season with salt and black pepper.

4 Cover and bake 40 minutes. Remove cover; bake 15 minutes or until chicken is cooked through (165°F).

BBQ CHICKEN SKILLET PIZZA

Makes 4 to 6 servings

1 loaf (1 pound) frozen bread dough, thawed

1 tablespoon olive oil

2 cups shredded cooked chicken*

¾ cup barbecue sauce, divided

¼ cup (1 ounce) shredded mozzarella cheese

¼ cup thinly sliced red onion

½ cup (2 ounces) shredded smoked Gouda

Chopped fresh cilantro (optional)

*Use a rotisserie chicken for best flavor and convenience.

1 Preheat oven to 425°F. Roll out dough into 15-inch circle on lightly floured surface. Brush oil over bottom and side of large (12-inch) cast iron skillet; place in oven 5 minutes to preheat.

2 Combine chicken and ½ cup barbecue sauce in medium bowl; toss to coat. Remove hot skillet from oven; press dough into bottom and about 1 inch up side of skillet.

3 Spread remaining ¼ cup barbecue sauce over dough. Sprinkle with mozzarella cheese; top with chicken mixture. Sprinkle with half of onion and Gouda cheese; top with remaining onion.

4 Bake 25 minutes or until crust is golden brown. Garnish with cilantro.

ITALIAN COUNTRY-STYLE BRAISED CHICKEN

Makes 4 to 6 servings

¾ cup boiling water

½ cup dried porcini mushrooms (about ½ ounce)

¼ cup all-purpose flour

1 teaspoon salt

½ teaspoon black pepper

1 cut-up whole chicken (3½ to 4 pounds)

3 tablespoons olive oil

2 ounces bacon or pancetta, chopped

1 medium onion, chopped

2 carrots, thinly sliced

3 cloves garlic, minced

1 cup chicken broth

1 tablespoon tomato paste

1 cup pitted green Italian olives

1 Combine boiling water and mushrooms in small bowl. Let stand 15 to 20 minutes or until mushrooms are tender.

2 Meanwhile, combine flour, salt and pepper in large resealable food storage bag. Add 1 or 2 pieces of chicken at a time; toss to coat. Discard any remaining flour mixture.

3 Heat 1 tablespoon oil in large skillet over medium heat. Add chicken in batches; cook 8 to 10 minutes or until browned on both sides. Remove chicken to plate; set aside. Repeat with remaining 2 tablespoons oil and chicken.

4 Pour off all but 1 tablespoon oil from skillet. Add bacon, onion and carrots; cook 5 minutes, stirring occasionally to scrape up browned bits. Add garlic; cook 1 minute.

5 Drain mushrooms, reserving liquid. Chop mushrooms. Add mushrooms and reserved liquid to skillet. Add broth and tomato paste; bring to a boil over high heat.

6 Return chicken to skillet with any juices from plate. Reduce heat to low; simmer 20 minutes or until chicken is cooked through (165°F) and sauce thickens, turning once. Stir in olives; cook and stir until heated through. Remove chicken to serving platter; top with sauce.

CHICKEN AND SHRIMP JAMBALAYA

Makes 4 servings

- 1 medium rutabaga, peeled
- 1 large onion
- 1 *each* red, yellow and green bell pepper
- 2½ to 3 cups chicken broth, divided
- ¾ teaspoon salt
- ⅛ teaspoon black pepper
- ⅛ teaspoon ground red pepper

- ½ pound boneless skinless chicken breast, cut into ½-inch pieces
- 1 tablespoon vegetable oil
- 2 cloves garlic, minced
- 1 large ripe tomato, chopped
- 6 ounces peeled and deveined medium shrimp (with tails on)
- 2 tablespoons chopped fresh parsley

1 Spiral rutabaga with thick spiral blade.* Place in food processor; pulse until chopped into rice-size pieces. Spiral onion with fine spiral blade; coarsely chop to shorten long pieces. Spiral bell peppers with spiral slice blade.

2 Bring 2 cups broth to a boil in medium saucepan. Add rutabaga rice; cook 5 to 7 minutes or until tender. Drain and return to saucepan; keep warm.

3 Meanwhile, combine salt, black pepper and red pepper in small bowl; sprinkle half of mixture over chicken. Heat oil in large nonstick skillet over medium heat. Add chicken; cook without stirring 2 minutes or until golden. Turn chicken; cook 2 minutes. Remove chicken to plate; set aside.

4 Add onion and bell peppers to same skillet; cook and stir 3 minutes or until onion is translucent. Add garlic; cook and stir 1 minute. Stir in chicken, tomato, shrimp, remaining spice mixture and ½ cup broth; bring to a boil. Reduce heat to low; cook 5 minutes or until shrimp are opaque.

5 Stir in parsley and rutabaga. Add additional broth if needed to moisten rice. Cook 3 minutes or until liquid is absorbed and jambalaya is heated through.

*If you don't have a spiralizer, cut the rutabaga into ribbons with a mandoline or sharp knife.

CHICKEN ADOBO

Makes 6 servings

½ cup cider vinegar

½ cup soy sauce

4 cloves garlic, minced

3 bay leaves

1 teaspoon black pepper

2½ pounds bone-in skin-on chicken thighs (about 6)

Hot cooked rice (optional)

Sliced green onion (optional)

1 Combine vinegar, soy sauce, garlic, bay leaves and pepper in large saucepan or deep skillet; mix well. Add chicken; turn to coat. Arrange chicken skin side down in liquid.

2 Bring to a boil over high heat. Reduce heat to low. Simmer, covered, 30 minutes. Turn chicken skin side up. Cook, uncovered, 20 minutes. Preheat broiler. Line small baking sheet with foil.

3 Remove chicken to prepared baking sheet, skin side up. Broil 6 minutes or until skin is browned and crisp. Meanwhile, cook liquid in saucepan over high heat 10 minutes or until reduced and slightly thickened.

4 Serve sauce over chicken and rice, if desired. Garnish with green onion.

CHEESY CHICKEN AND BACON

Makes 4 servings

½ cup Dijon mustard

4 tablespoons olive oil, divided

1 teaspoon lemon juice

4 boneless skinless chicken breasts (about 6 ounces each)

Salt and black pepper

1 tablespoon butter

2 cups sliced mushrooms

4 slices bacon, crisp-cooked

½ cup (2 ounces) shredded Cheddar cheese

½ cup (2 ounces) shredded Monterey Jack cheese

Chopped fresh parsley

1 Whisk mustard, 3 tablespoons oil and lemon juice in medium bowl until well blended. Remove half of marinade mixture to use as sauce; cover and refrigerate until ready to serve.

2 Place chicken in large resealable food storage bag. Pour remaining half of marinade over chicken; seal bag and turn to coat. Refrigerate at least 2 hours.

3 Preheat oven to 375°F. Remove chicken from marinade; discard marinade. Heat remaining 1 tablespoon oil in large ovenproof skillet over medium-high heat. Add chicken; cook 3 to 4 minutes per side or until golden brown. (Chicken will not be cooked through.) Remove chicken to plate; sprinkle with salt and pepper.

4 Heat butter in same skillet over medium-high heat. Add mushrooms; cook 8 minutes or until mushrooms begin to brown, stirring occasionally and scraping up browned bits from bottom of skillet. Season with salt and pepper. Return chicken to skillet; spoon mushrooms over chicken. Top with bacon; sprinkle with Cheddar and Monterey Jack cheeses.

5 Bake 8 to 10 minutes or until chicken is no longer pink in center and cheeses are melted. Sprinkle with parsley; serve with reserved mustard mixture.

LEMON-PEPPER CHICKEN

Makes 4 servings

⅓ cup lemon juice

¼ cup finely chopped onion

2 tablespoons olive oil

1 tablespoon packed brown sugar

1 tablespoon black pepper

3 cloves garlic, minced

2 teaspoons grated lemon peel

½ teaspoon salt

4 boneless skinless chicken breasts (about 1 pound)

1 Combine lemon juice, onion, oil, brown sugar, pepper, garlic, lemon peel and salt in small bowl; stir to blend. Pour marinade over chicken in large resealable food storage bag. Seal bag; knead to coat. Refrigerate at least 4 hours or overnight.

2 Prepare grill for direct cooking over medium heat.

3 Remove chicken from marinade; discard marinade. Grill, covered, 15 to 20 minutes or until chicken is cooked through (165°F) and no longer pink in center.

BRUSCHETTA CHICKEN FETTUCCINE

Makes 4 servings

Balsamic Glaze

- ¼ cup balsamic vinegar
- 2 tablespoons packed brown sugar
- 1 teaspoon molasses
- ¼ teaspoon salt

Bruschetta Sauce

- 4 cups diced plum tomatoes (about 4 medium)
- ½ cup tomato sauce
- ¼ cup olive oil
- ¼ cup chopped fresh basil
- 1 tablespoon white wine vinegar
- 2 cloves garlic, minced
- ¾ teaspoon salt
- ½ teaspoon black pepper

Chicken

- 4 boneless skinless chicken breasts (4 ounces each)
  Salt and black pepper
- ¼ teaspoon garlic powder
- 1 tablespoon olive oil
- 1 package (16 ounces) uncooked fettuccine
- ¼ cup grated Parmesan cheese
  Shaved Parmesan (optional)
  Chopped fresh parsley (optional)

1 For glaze, combine balsamic vinegar, brown sugar, molasses and ¼ teaspoon salt in small saucepan; bring to a simmer over medium heat. Cook 10 minutes or until reduced by half. Set aside to cool.

2 For sauce, combine tomatoes, tomato sauce, ¼ cup oil, basil, white wine vinegar, garlic, ¾ teaspoon salt and ½ teaspoon pepper in medium bowl; mix well.

3 If necessary, pound chicken to ¾-inch thickness between two sheets of waxed paper or plastic wrap with rolling pin or meat mallet. Season with salt, pepper and garlic powder. Heat 1 tablespoon oil in large skillet over medium-high heat. Add chicken; cook 5 minutes per side or until golden brown and cooked through (165°F). Remove to plate; cover loosely with foil to keep warm.

4 Meanwhile, cook pasta in large saucepan of salted boiling water according to package directions until al dente. Drain in colander; return empty saucepan to stove. Add sauce

to saucepan; cook and stir over high heat 2 minutes or until heated through. Add pasta and grated Parmesan to saucepan; toss to coat.

5 Slice chicken. Divide pasta among four serving bowls; drizzle with glaze. Top each serving with sliced chicken breast; garnish with shaved Parmesan and parsley. Serve immediately.

SIMPLE ROASTED CHICKEN

Makes 4 servings

1 whole chicken (about 4 pounds)

3 tablespoons butter, softened

1½ teaspoons salt

1 teaspoon onion powder

1 teaspoon dried thyme

½ teaspoon garlic powder

½ teaspoon paprika

½ teaspoon black pepper

12 unpeeled small red potatoes, halved (about ¾ pound)

8 ounces sliced mushrooms

Fresh basil leaves (optional)

1 Preheat oven to 425°F. Pat chicken dry; place in small baking dish or on baking sheet.

2 Combine butter, salt, onion powder, thyme, garlic powder, paprika and pepper in small microwavable bowl; mash with fork until well blended. Loosen skin on breasts and thighs; spread about one third of butter mixture under skin.

3 Microwave remaining butter mixture until melted. Brush melted butter mixture all over outside of chicken and inside cavity. Tie drumsticks together with kitchen string and tuck wing tips under.

4 Roast 20 minutes. Add potatoes and mushrooms. *Reduce oven temperature to 375°F.* Roast 45 to 55 minutes or until chicken is cooked through (165°F), basting once with pan juices during last 10 minutes of cooking time. Remove chicken, potatoes and mushrooms to large serving platter; tent with foil. Let stand at least 15 minutes before carving. Garnish with basil.

OVEN BARBECUE CHICKEN

Makes 4 to 6 servings

1 cup barbecue sauce

¼ cup honey

2 tablespoons soy sauce

2 teaspoons grated fresh ginger

½ teaspoon dry mustard

1 cut-up whole chicken (about 3½ pounds)

1 Preheat oven to 350°F. Combine barbecue sauce, honey, soy sauce, ginger and mustard in small bowl; mix well.

2 Place chicken in lightly greased baking dish. Brush evenly with sauce mixture. Bake 45 minutes or until cooked through (165°F), brushing occasionally with sauce.

BEER CHICKEN

Makes 4 servings

1⅓ cups light-colored beer, such as pale ale

2 tablespoons buttermilk

1¼ cups panko bread crumbs

½ cup grated Parmesan cheese

4 chicken breast cutlets (about 1¼ pounds)

Salt and black pepper

1 Preheat oven to 400°F. Line large baking sheet with foil.

2 Combine beer and buttermilk in shallow bowl. Combine panko and cheese in another shallow bowl. Sprinkle chicken with salt and pepper. Dip in beer mixture; roll in panko mixture to coat. Place on prepared baking sheet.

3 Bake 25 to 30 minutes or until chicken is no longer pink in center.

TIP: To make a substitution for buttermilk, place 1 teaspoon lemon juice or distilled white vinegar in a measuring cup and add enough milk to measure 2 tablespoons. Stir and let the mixture stand at room temperature for 5 minutes. Discard leftover mixture.

Oven Barbecue
Chicken

CHICKEN MARSALA

Makes 4 servings

- 4 boneless, skinless chicken breasts
- 2 tablespoons all-purpose flour
- ½ teaspoon salt
- ½ teaspoon SPICE ISLANDS® Garlic Powder
- ¼ teaspoon SPICE ISLANDS® Fine Grind Black Pepper
- 3 tablespoons olive oil, divided

- 1 cup sliced fresh mushrooms
- 2 teaspoons ARGO® Corn Starch
- ½ cup Marsala wine
- ½ cup chicken broth
- ½ teaspoon SPICE ISLANDS® Sweet Basil
- ½ teaspoon SPICE ISLANDS® Onion Powder
- Cooked linguine (optional)

POUND chicken pieces to ¼-inch thickness (place between 2 sheets of waxed paper).

COMBINE flour, salt, garlic powder and pepper in a large bowl. Add chicken; coat with flour mixture.

HEAT 2 tablespoons oil in large skillet over medium-high heat. Cook chicken 8 to 10 minutes, or until done, turning once. Remove from pan.

ADD 1 tablespoon oil and mushrooms to skillet. Sauté 2 to 3 minutes. Mix corn starch, wine, broth, basil and onion powder until well blended; add to mushrooms. Simmer, uncovered, 2 minutes or until thickened.

SERVE chicken and sauce over linguine, if desired.

CRISPY RANCH CHICKEN

Makes 6 servings

1½ cups cornflake crumbs	½ teaspoon black pepper
1 teaspoon dried rosemary	1½ cups ranch salad dressing
½ teaspoon salt	3 pounds chicken pieces

1 Preheat oven to 375°F. Spray 13×9-inch baking dish with nonstick cooking spray. Combine cornflakes, rosemary, salt and pepper in medium bowl.

2 Pour salad dressing in separate medium bowl. Dip chicken pieces in salad dressing, coating well. Dredge coated chicken in crumb mixture. Place in prepared baking dish.

3 Bake 50 to 55 minutes or until cooked through (165°F).

VARIATION: To add an Italian flair to this dish, try substituting 1¼ cups Italian-seasoned dry bread crumbs and ¼ cup grated Parmesan cheese for the cornflake crumbs, rosemary, salt and pepper. Prepare recipe as directed.

BISTRO CHICKEN IN RICH CREAM SAUCE

Makes 4 servings

4 skinless, bone-in chicken breasts, rinsed and patted dry (about 3 pounds total)

½ cup dry white wine, divided

1 tablespoon or ½ packet (0.7 ounces) Italian salad dressing and seasoning mix

½ teaspoon dried oregano

1 can (10¾ ounces) cream of chicken soup

3 ounces cream cheese, cut into cubes

¼ teaspoon salt

⅛ teaspoon black pepper

2 tablespoons chopped fresh parsley

Slow Cooker Directions

1 Coat 6-quart slow cooker with nonstick cooking spray. Arrange chicken in single layer in bottom, overlapping slightly. Pour ¼ cup wine over chicken. Sprinkle evenly with salad dressing mix and oregano. Cover; cook on LOW 5 to 6 hours or on HIGH 3 hours.

2 Remove chicken to plate with slotted spoon. Whisk soup, cream cheese, salt and pepper into cooking liquid. (Mixture will be a bit lumpy.) Arrange chicken on top. Cover; cook on HIGH 15 to 20 minutes or until heated through.

3 Remove chicken to shallow pasta bowl. Add remaining ¼ cup wine to sauce and whisk until smooth. To serve, spoon sauce around chicken. Garnish with parsley.

CHICKEN CACCIATORE

Makes 4 to 6 servings

1 tablespoon olive oil

1 broiler-fryer chicken (3 to 3½ pounds), cut into 8 pieces

4 ounces mushrooms, finely chopped

1 medium onion, chopped

1 clove garlic, minced

½ cup dry white wine

1 tablespoon plus 1½ teaspoons white wine vinegar

½ cup chicken broth

1 teaspoon dried basil

½ teaspoon dried marjoram

½ teaspoon salt

⅛ teaspoon black pepper

1 can (about 14 ounces) whole tomatoes, undrained

8 Italian- or Greek-style pitted black olives, halved

1 tablespoon chopped fresh parsley

Hot cooked pasta

1 Heat oil in large skillet over medium heat. Add as many chicken pieces in single layer without crowding. Cook 8 minutes per side or until chicken is brown; remove chicken with slotted spatula to Dutch oven. Repeat with remaining chicken pieces.

2 Add mushrooms and onion to drippings in skillet. Cook and stir over medium heat 5 minutes or until onion is soft. Add garlic; cook and stir 30 seconds. Add wine and vinegar; cook over medium-high heat 5 minutes or until liquid is almost evaporated. Stir in broth, basil, marjoram, salt and pepper. Remove from heat.

3 Press tomatoes with juice through sieve into onion mixture; discard seeds. Bring to a boil over medium-high heat; boil, uncovered, 2 minutes. Pour tomato-onion mixture over chicken. Bring to a boil; reduce heat to low. Cover and simmer 25 minutes or until chicken is tender and juices run clear when pierced with fork. Remove chicken with slotted spatula to heated serving dish; keep warm.

4 Bring tomato-onion sauce to a boil over medium-high heat; boil, uncovered, 5 minutes. Add olives and parsley; cook 1 minute. Pour sauce over chicken and pasta.

GREEK CHICKEN BURGERS WITH CUCUMBER YOGURT SAUCE

Makes 4 servings

½ cup plus 2 tablespoons plain Greek yogurt

½ medium cucumber, peeled, seeded and finely chopped

Juice of ½ lemon

3 cloves garlic, minced, divided

2 teaspoons finely chopped fresh mint *or* ½ teaspoon dried mint

⅛ teaspoon salt

⅛ teaspoon ground white pepper

1 pound ground chicken

¾ cup (3 ounces) crumbled feta cheese

4 large kalamata olives, rinsed, patted dry and minced

1 egg

½ to 1 teaspoon dried oregano

¼ teaspoon black pepper

Mixed baby lettuce (optional)

Fresh mint leaves (optional)

1 Combine yogurt, cucumber, lemon juice, 2 cloves garlic, 2 teaspoons chopped mint, salt and white pepper in medium bowl; mix well. Cover and refrigerate until ready to serve.

2 Combine chicken, cheese, olives, egg, oregano, black pepper and remaining 1 clove garlic in large bowl; mix well. Shape mixture into four patties.

3 Spray grill pan with nonstick cooking spray; heat over medium-high heat. Grill patties 5 to 7 minutes per side or until cooked through (165°F).

4 Serve burgers with sauce and mixed greens, if desired. Garnish with mint leaves.

WAFFLED CHICKEN SALTIMBOCCA

Makes 4 servings

4 boneless skinless chicken breasts (about 4 ounces each)

Kosher salt

Freshly ground black pepper

4 large fresh sage leaves

4 slices prosciutto

1 tablespoon vegetable oil

1 Preheat classic waffle maker to high heat.

2 Season chicken on both sides with salt and pepper. Place sage leaf in center of each chicken breast.

3 Working one chicken breast at a time, wrap one slice prosciutto around center third of chicken so it covers the leaf completely. Brush prosciutto-wrapped chicken on both sides with oil. Repeat with remaining chicken.

4 Place two of the prepared chicken breasts side-by-side on waffle maker; close lid. Cook 5 minutes or until chicken is opaque and firm. Remove to plate; tent with foil to keep warm. Repeat with remaining chicken.

15-MINUTE CHICKEN & RICE DINNER

Makes 4 servings

1¼ pounds skinless, boneless chicken breast halves

1 tablespoon vegetable oil

1 can (10½ ounces) CAMPBELL'S® Condensed Cream of Chicken Soup or CAMPBELL'S® Condensed 98% Fat Free Cream of Chicken Soup

1½ cups water

¼ teaspoon paprika

¼ teaspoon ground black pepper

2 cups **uncooked** instant white rice

2 cups fresh **or** frozen broccoli florets

1 Season the chicken as desired. Heat the oil in a 12-inch skillet over medium-high heat. Add the chicken and cook for 10 minutes or until well browned on both sides. Remove the chicken from the skillet.

2 Stir the soup, water, paprika and black pepper in the skillet and heat to a boil. Stir in the rice and broccoli. Reduce the heat to low. Return the chicken to the skillet. Sprinkle the chicken with additional paprika. Cover and cook for 5 minutes or until the chicken is cooked through. Season to taste.

EASY SUBSTITUTION: This recipe is also delicious using CAMPBELL'S® Condensed Cream of Mushroom Soup instead of the Cream of Chicken.

RECIPE NOTE: For a creamier dish, decrease the rice to 1½ cups.

INGREDIENT NOTE: We develop our recipes using a 4- to 5-ounce skinless, boneless chicken breast half per serving. However, there are a range of sizes available in-store, from the butcher counter to the meat case and the freezer section. Use whichever you prefer-just follow the recipe as written above for the best result. If you're using larger chicken breasts they may require a little longer cooking time.

GREEK CHICKEN AND ARTICHOKE RICE

Makes 4 servings

2 tablespoons olive oil, divided

1 pound chicken tenders

Paprika

¼ cup pine nuts

2 cups chicken broth

1 can (about 14 ounces) artichoke heart quarters, drained

1 cup uncooked rice

1½ tablespoons grated lemon peel

1 medium clove garlic

½ teaspoon salt, divided

⅛ teaspoon black pepper

Juice of 1 medium lemon

2 tablespoons chopped fresh parsley

2 ounces feta cheese with sun-dried tomatoes and basil, crumbled

1 Heat 1 tablespoon oil in large skillet over medium-high heat. Sprinkle chicken lightly with paprika. Add chicken to skillet; cook 2 minutes on one side. Remove from skillet; set aside.

2 Add pine nuts to skillet; cook 1 minute or until golden brown, stirring constantly. Add broth, artichokes, rice, lemon peel, garlic, ¼ teaspoon salt and pepper. Return chicken to skillet, seasoned side up; press down gently into rice mixture. Bring to a boil. Reduce heat; cover and simmer 15 minutes or until rice is tender.

3 Remove from heat. Drizzle with lemon juice and remaining 1 tablespoon oil. Sprinkle with remaining ¼ teaspoon salt, parsley and cheese. *Do not stir.* Serve immediately.

MIDDLE EASTERN CHICKEN

Makes 4 servings

1 pound boneless skinless chicken breasts, cut into 1×½-inch pieces

1 can (about 14 ounces) diced tomatoes

1¼ cups chicken broth

¼ package dry onion soup mix (about 1 tablespoon)

2 tablespoons tomato paste

1 can (14 ounces) artichoke hearts, drained and quartered (about 1 cup)

¼ cup sliced black olives

¼ teaspoon ground allspice

¼ teaspoon ground cinnamon

1 Spray large skillet with nonstick cooking spray; heat over medium-high heat. Add chicken; cook 2 minutes or until lightly browned.

2 Stir in tomatoes, broth, dry soup mix and tomato paste. Bring to a boil; reduce heat to low and simmer 20 minutes.

3 Add artichokes, olives, allspice and cinnamon; stir. Simmer 3 minutes or until chicken is cooked through.

SERVING SUGGESTIONS: Serve with whole wheat pita triangles and mixed baby greens salad.

CHICKEN AND VEGGIE FAJITAS

Makes 6 servings

1 pound boneless skinless chicken thighs, cut crosswise into strips

1 teaspoon dried oregano

1 teaspoon chili powder

½ teaspoon garlic salt

2 bell peppers (preferably 1 red and 1 green), cut into thin strips

4 thin slices large sweet or yellow onion, separated into rings

½ cup salsa

6 (6-inch) flour tortillas, warmed

½ cup chopped fresh cilantro or green onions

Sour cream (optional)

1 Toss chicken with oregano, chili powder and garlic salt in large bowl. Heat large skillet coated with nonstick cooking spray over medium-high heat. Add chicken; cook and stir 5 to 6 minutes or until cooked through. Remove to bowl; set aside.

2 Add bell peppers and onion to same skillet; cook and stir 2 minutes over medium heat. Add salsa; cover and cook 6 to 8 minutes or until vegetables are tender. Uncover; stir in chicken and any juices from bowl. Cook and stir 2 minutes or until heated through.

3 Serve mixture on top of tortillas topped with cilantro and sour cream, if desired.

SOUTHWESTERN CHICKEN AND BLACK BEAN SKILLET

Makes 4 servings

1 teaspoon ground cumin

1 teaspoon chili powder

½ teaspoon salt

4 boneless skinless chicken breasts (about 1 pound)

2 teaspoons canola or vegetable oil

1 cup chopped onion

1 red bell pepper, chopped

1 can (about 15 ounces) black beans, rinsed and drained

½ cup chunky salsa

¼ cup chopped fresh cilantro or thinly sliced green onions (optional)

1 Combine cumin, chili powder and salt in small bowl; sprinkle evenly over both sides of chicken.

2 Heat oil in large skillet over medium-high heat. Add chicken; cook 4 minutes, turning once. Remove to plate.

3 Add onion to same skillet; cook and stir 1 minute. Add bell pepper; cook 5 minutes, stirring occasionally. Stir in beans and salsa.

4 Place chicken on top of bean mixture. Cover; cook 6 to 7 minutes or until chicken is no longer pink in center. Garnish with cilantro.

SKILLET CHICKEN CREOLE

Makes 4 servings

1 small red onion, chopped

1 small red bell pepper, chopped

1 jalapeño pepper, seeded and minced

2 cups canned crushed tomatoes

¼ teaspoon salt

⅛ teaspoon black pepper

12 ounces boneless skinless chicken breasts, cut into strips

Hot cooked white rice (optional)

1 Spray large skillet with nonstick cooking spray; heat over medium heat. Add onion, bell pepper and jalapeño; cook over medium heat 5 to 10 minutes or until vegetables are tender, stirring frequently. Stir in crushed tomatoes, salt and black pepper.

2 Stir in chicken. Reduce heat to low; cover and simmer 12 to 15 minutes or until chicken is cooked through. Serve over rice, if desired.

NOTE: If jalapeño pepper is too mild-tasting, add ¼ teaspoon red pepper flakes.

FAJITA-SEASONED CHICKEN

Makes 2 servings

- 2 boneless skinless chicken breasts (about 4 ounces each)
- 1 bunch green onions, ends trimmed

- 1 tablespoon olive oil
- 2 teaspoons fajita seasoning mix

1 Prepare grill for direct cooking.

2 Brush chicken and green onions with oil. Sprinkle both sides of chicken breasts with seasoning mix. Grill chicken and green onions 6 to 8 minutes or until chicken is no longer pink in center. Serve chicken with green onions.

SALSA VERDE CHICKEN TACOS

Makes 4 servings

- 1 pound diced skinless, boneless chicken breast halves
- 1 tablespoon vegetable oil
- 1 cup Pace® Salsa Verde
- 1 small avocado, pitted, peeled and diced (about ½ cup)

- 1 teaspoon lime juice
- 1 medium red bell pepper, diced (about ½ cup)
- ½ cup sour cream
- 8 flour tortillas (6-inch) or taco shells, warmed

1 Season the chicken as desired. Heat the oil in a 12-inch skillet over medium-high heat. Add the chicken and cook for 5 minutes or until well browned and cooked through, stirring occasionally. Stir in ½ cup salsa verde and cook until hot.

2 Place the avocado into a medium bowl. Add the lime juice and toss to coat.

3 Divide the chicken mixture, pepper, avocado mixture, sour cream and remaining ½ cup salsa verde among the tortillas. Fold the tortillas around the filling.

Fajita—Seasoned
Chicken

EASY CAJUN CHICKEN STEW

Makes 4 servings

2 tablespoons vegetable oil

1 red bell pepper, diced

1 stalk celery, sliced

1 can (about 14 ounces) diced tomatoes with roasted garlic and onions

1½ cups chicken broth

1 package (about 10 ounces) refrigerated fully cooked chicken breast strips, cut into pieces

1 pouch (about 9 ounces) New Orleans-style chicken-flavored ready-to-serve rice mix

1 cup canned kidney beans, rinsed and drained

¼ teaspoon hot pepper sauce

¼ cup chopped green onions

1 Heat oil in large saucepan or Dutch oven over medium-high heat. Add bell pepper and celery; cook and stir 3 minutes. Add tomatoes and broth; bring to a boil.

2 Add chicken, rice mix, beans and hot pepper sauce. Reduce heat to low. Cover; cook 7 minutes. Stir in green onions. Remove from heat. Cover; let stand 2 to 3 minutes to thicken.

TIP: If canned diced tomatoes with garlic and onions are not available, substitute 1 can (about 14 ounces) diced tomatoes, ¼ cup chopped onion and 1 teaspoon minced garlic.

ALMOND CHICKEN CUPS

Makes 12 chicken cups

- 1 tablespoon vegetable oil
- ½ cup chopped onion
- ½ cup chopped red bell pepper
- 2 cups chopped cooked chicken
- ⅔ cup prepared sweet and sour sauce
- ½ cup chopped almonds
- 2 tablespoons soy sauce
- 6 (6- to 7-inch) flour tortillas

1. Preheat oven to 400°F. Heat oil in small skillet over medium heat. Add onion and bell pepper; cook and stir 3 minutes or until crisp-tender.

2. Combine vegetable mixture, chicken, sweet and sour sauce, almonds and soy sauce in medium bowl; mix well.

3. Cut each tortilla in half. Place each half in standard (2¾-inch) muffin cup. Fill each with about ¼ cup chicken mixture.

4. Bake 8 to 10 minutes or until tortilla edges are crisp and filling is heated through. Cool on wire rack 5 minutes before serving.

QUICK CREAMY CHICKEN & NOODLES

Makes 4 servings

1 can (10½ ounces) CAMPBELL'S® Condensed Cream of Chicken and Mushroom Soup

½ cup milk

⅛ teaspoon ground black pepper

⅓ cup grated Parmesan cheese

2 cups cubed cooked boneless, skinless chicken breast

3 cups cooked egg noodles (from 4 ounces/about 3 cups dry)

1 tablespoon chopped fresh parsley

Heat the soup, milk, black pepper, cheese, chicken and noodles in a 4-quart saucepan over medium heat until the mixture is hot and bubbling, stirring occasionally. Season to taste. Sprinkle with the parsley before serving.

EASY SUBSTITUTION: Substitute 3 cans (4.5 ounces **each**) SWANSON® Premium White Chunk Chicken Breast in Water, drained, for the cooked chicken.

PANHANDLE PEPPERONI CHICKEN

Makes 4 servings

1 tablespoon olive oil

1 pound skinless, boneless chicken breast halves (about 4 breast halves)

1 cup PACE® Picante Sauce-Medium

1 teaspoon Italian seasoning, crushed

1 medium green pepper, cut into 1-inch pieces (about 1 cup)

1¼ ounces chopped pepperoni (about ⅓ cup)

4 tablespoons shredded part skim mozzarella cheese (optional)

1 cup regular long grain white rice, cooked according to package directions (about 3 cups)

1 Heat the oil in a 10-inch skillet over medium-high heat. Add the chicken and cook for 10 minutes or until it's well browned on both sides. Remove the chicken from the skillet and set aside.

2 Stir the picante sauce, Italian seasoning, green pepper and pepperoni in the skillet and heat to a boil. Return chicken to the skillet. Reduce the heat to low. Cover and cook for 5 minutes or until the chicken is cooked through. Garnish with the cheese and serve with the rice.

CREAMY CHICKEN QUESADILLAS

Makes 6 servings

1 can (10½ ounces) CAMPBELL'S® Condensed Cream of Chicken Soup or CAMPBELL'S® Condensed 98% Fat Free Cream of Chicken Soup

1 cup shredded Cheddar cheese (about 4 ounces)

1 jalapeño pepper, seeded and finely chopped (optional)

2 cans (4.5 ounces **each**) SWANSON® Premium White Chunk Chicken Breast in Water, drained

8 flour tortillas (8-inch), warmed

½ cup PACE® Chunky Salsa-Mild

½ cup sour cream

1 Heat the oven to 400°F. Stir the soup, ½ cup cheese, jalapeño pepper, if desired, and chicken in a medium bowl.

2 Place the tortillas onto 2 baking sheets. Spread ¼ cup chicken mixture on half of each tortilla to within ½ inch of the edge. Brush the edges of the tortillas with water. Fold the tortillas over the filling and press the edges to seal.

3 Bake for 10 minutes or until the filling is hot. Sprinkle with the remaining cheese. Serve with the salsa and sour cream.

EASY SUBSTITUTION: Substitute 1½ cups chopped cooked chicken for the SWANSON® Chicken.

SOY GINGER CHICKEN

Makes 4 servings

1¼ pounds skinless, boneless chicken breast halves

1 tablespoon vegetable oil **or** olive oil

½ cup water

1 can (10½ ounces) CAMPBELL'S® Condensed Cream of Mushroom Soup **or** CAMPBELL'S® Healthy Request® Condensed Healthy Request® Cream of Mushroom Soup

1 tablespoon creamy peanut butter

1 tablespoon soy sauce

½ teaspoon ground ginger

1 tablespoon chopped fresh cilantro

1 Season the chicken. Heat the oil in a 10-inch skillet over medium-high heat. (Make sure the skillet and oil are hot before adding the chicken—it will jump start the browning and prevent the chicken from sticking.) Add the chicken and cook for at least 3 minutes before turning (if it doesn't turn easily give it another minute on that side) then cook until both sides are well browned. Remove the chicken from the skillet.

2 Add the water to the skillet and heat to a boil, stirring to scrape up the browned bits from the bottom of the skillet. Stir in the soup, peanut butter, soy sauce and ginger and heat to a boil.

3 Return the chicken to the skillet. Reduce the heat to medium-low. Cover and cook for 5 minutes or until the chicken is cooked through. Season to taste. Sprinkle with the cilantro before serving.

RECIPE TIP: For extra heat, drizzle with 2 teaspoons sriracha sauce before serving.

SERVING SUGGESTION: Serve over hot cooked noodles or jasmine rice.

INDEX

Acknowledgments
The publisher would like to thank the companies and organizations
listed below for the use of their recipes and photographs in this publication.

ACH Food Companies, Inc.
Campbell Soup Company
Ortega®, A Division of B&G Foods North America, Inc.
Riviana Foods Inc.
Unilever

METRIC CONVERSION CHART

VOLUME MEASUREMENTS (dry)

$1/8$ teaspoon = 0.5 mL
$1/4$ teaspoon = 1 mL
$1/2$ teaspoon = 2 mL
$3/4$ teaspoon = 4 mL
1 teaspoon = 5 mL
1 tablespoon = 15 mL
2 tablespoons = 30 mL
$1/4$ cup = 60 mL
$1/3$ cup = 75 mL
$1/2$ cup = 125 mL
$2/3$ cup = 150 mL
$3/4$ cup = 175 mL
1 cup = 250 mL
2 cups = 1 pint = 500 mL
3 cups = 750 mL
4 cups = 1 quart = 1 L

VOLUME MEASUREMENTS (fluid)

1 fluid ounce (2 tablespoons) = 30 mL
4 fluid ounces ($1/2$ cup) = 125 mL
8 fluid ounces (1 cup) = 250 mL
12 fluid ounces ($1 1/2$ cups) = 375 mL
16 fluid ounces (2 cups) = 500 mL

WEIGHTS (mass)

$1/2$ ounce = 15 g
1 ounce = 30 g
3 ounces = 90 g
4 ounces = 120 g
8 ounces = 225 g
10 ounces = 285 g
12 ounces = 360 g
16 ounces = 1 pound = 450 g

DIMENSIONS

$1/16$ inch = 2 mm
$1/8$ inch = 3 mm
$1/4$ inch = 6 mm
$1/2$ inch = 1.5 cm
$3/4$ inch = 2 cm
1 inch = 2.5 cm

OVEN TEMPERATURES

250°F = 120°C
275°F = 140°C
300°F = 150°C
325°F = 160°C
350°F = 180°C
375°F = 190°C
400°F = 200°C
425°F = 220°C
450°F = 230°C

BAKING PAN SIZES

Utensil	Size in Inches/Quarts	Metric Volume	Size in Centimeters
Baking or Cake Pan (square or rectangular)	8×8×2	2 L	20×20×5
	9×9×2	2.5 L	23×23×5
	12×8×2	3 L	30×20×5
	13×9×2	3.5 L	33×23×5
Loaf Pan	8×4×3	1.5 L	20×10×7
	9×5×3	2 L	23×13×7
Round Layer Cake Pan	8×1½	1.2 L	20×4
	9×1½	1.5 L	23×4
Pie Plate	8×1¼	750 mL	20×3
	9×1¼	1 L	23×3
Baking Dish or Casserole	1 quart	1 L	—
	1½ quart	1.5 L	—
	2 quart	2 L	—